# The Amazing Stitching HANDBOOK for Kids

**17** Embroidery Stitches

**15** Fun & Easy Projects

## Kristin Nicholas

FunStitch
**STUDIO**
stitch your art out.

Text copyright and artwork copyright © 2015 by Kristin Nicholas

Photography and illustrations copyright © 2015 by C&T Publishing, Inc.

**Publisher:** Amy Marson

**Creative Director:** Gailen Runge

**Art Director/Cover Designer:** Kristy Zacharias

**Editor:** S. Michele Fry

**Technical Editors:** Ann Haley and Gailen Runge

**Book Designer:** April Mostek

**Production Coordinator:** Jenny Davis

**Production Editor:** Joanna Burgarino

**Illustrator:** Mary E. Flynn

**Photo Assistant:** Mary Peyton Peppo

**Style photography** by Nissa Brehmer and **instructional photography** by Diane Pedersen, unless otherwise noted

Published by FunStitch Studio, an imprint of C&T Publishing, Inc., P.O. Box 1456, Lafayette, CA 94549

Library of Congress Cataloging-in-Publication Data

Nicholas, Kristin.

The amazing stitching handbook for kids : 17 embroidery stitches :15 fun & easy projects / Kristin Nicholas.

pages cm

ISBN 978-1-60705-973-8 (soft cover)

1. Embroidery--Juvenile literature.  I. Title.

TT770.5.N528 2015

746.44--dc23

2014043401

Printed in Malaysia

10 9 8 7 6 5 4 3

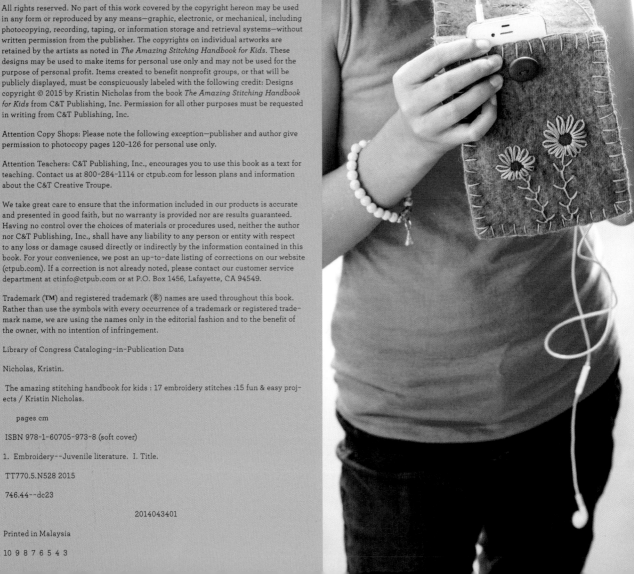

# Contents

DEDICATION  4

ACKNOWLEDGMENTS  4

INTRODUCTION  5

EMBROIDERY TOOLS  6
*Fabric · Thread and Yarn · Needles*

## Gridded Stitches  18

NEEDLEPOINT  19
*Tent Stitch · Edge Stitch*

Projects:
Striped Coasters  24
Stitch-It Photo Frame  28

CROSS-STITCH  33
*Cross-Stitch on Gingham*

Project:
Cross-Stitch Dish Towels  35

## Basic Free-Form Embroidery  38

*Running Stitch · Seed Stitch · Backstitch ·
Stem Stitch · Satin Stitch · Straight Stitch ·
Whipstitch*

Projects:
Needlebook  48
Sew Pincushion  52
Backpack Tags  55
Love Heart Pillow  57
Owl Stuffie  60

## Looped Stitches  66

*Blanket Stitch · Chain Stitch ·
Lazy Daisy · Featherstitch*

Projects:
Bookmarks  75
Dots Hoop Art  77
Embroidered Blue Jeans  81
Phone or MP3 Player Cozy  85
Embellished Fabric Picture  90

## Fancy Stitches  96

*French Knots · Bullion Knot ·
Spider Web Stitch · Woven Bar*

Projects:
Tess's Notecard  103
Embellished Carry Tote  108
Patch Collection  111

HOW TO MAKE IT YOURS  116
*Stitch Guide · Motifs · Embroidery Ideas*

GLOSSARY  119

PATTERNS AND MOTIFS  120

SOURCES FOR SUPPLIES  127

ABOUT THE AUTHOR  127

# Dedication

*For my grandmother Frieda Röessler Nicholas, and for all of the grandmothers who encourage their grandchildren to follow their dreams.*

# Acknowledgments

Embroidery has been around for thousands of years. I learned to stitch from my mom, **Nancy Nicholas**, when she first placed a Sunset Stitchery kit in my hands in the 1970s. Back then, I fell in love with the rhythm, creativity, and texture of the stitching. Thank you, Mom, for starting me on my journey.

I dabble in many crafts, but embroidery has always been one of my favorites. The first edition of *Kids' Embroidery* was published in 2004 by Stewart, Tabori, and Chang and was edited by **Melanie Falick**, and to her I am grateful for the chance to bring embroidery to the hands of many young people over a decade ago. As time has passed, there has been a revolution in the DIY culture. Through blogs and the Internet, hand embroidery is experiencing a rebirth. More and more people, young and old, are picking up needle and thread and creating their own art with stitches.

I am so happy that *The Amazing Stitching Handbook for Kids* is available in this new updated edition with new projects. Thank you to the folks at **C&T Publishing** for bringing it back to life and passing embroidery on to a new generation of stitchers. Thank you, **Michele Fry** and **Ann Haley**, for your editing. Thank you, **Nissa Brehmer** and **Diane Pedersen**, for your photos.

Thanks go to **Linda Roghaar**, my agent, who believed in the book and was able to find it a second home. Thanks to all of the companies that contributed supplies, especially **A Child's Dream**. Thank you to **Tess Vreeland** for stitching your blue jeans.

Last, thank you to Mark, my husband, and Julia, our daughter, who support and entertain me, and most of all, lived through the creative chaos.

# Introduction

**TO EMBROIDER MEANS TO EMBELLISH, OR DECORATE, A PIECE OF FABRIC WITH A NEEDLE AND THREAD.** It's really just fancy sewing. In *The Amazing Stitching Handbook for Kids*, you will discover many ways to have fun. You can work on a grid and do needlepoint or cross-stitch, or you can work in a less structured way and do free-form embroidery, which is a lot like drawing. People have been embroidering all over the world for thousands of years.

This book shows many different projects—a stuffie, iPod carrying case (a cozy!), ornaments, coasters, pincushions, bags, bookmarks, and more. **MOST OF THEM ONLY TAKE A COUPLE OF HOURS TO COMPLETE.** You can start using scrap fabric to learn the basic stitches shown at the beginning of each chapter, or you can jump right into the projects and learn as you go.

If you don't want to make the exact projects you see here, make them your own way. For example, use the motif (design) and stitches shown on something else. Add personal designs to clothes. Create decoration. You can embellish almost anything! Embroidery can be done on any surface—baskets, purses, backpacks, notebooks, even lampshades. The only requirement is that you be able to poke a threaded needle through the item. So while a wooden box won't work, a cardboard box will!

When you begin embroidering, **DON'T WORRY ABOUT BEING PERFECT.** As you practice, your stitching will naturally improve. In no time, the stitches will be neat and even. When you look back at your first projects, you will probably love—or at least laugh at—any strange-looking stitches. Amazingly, each time you touch a piece of embroidery you have made, you will remember where you were and what was happening in your life at that time. If you embroider gifts for family members or friends, they are sure to treasure them. There's really nothing like something handmade to show people that you think they're special.

**YOU CAN EMBROIDER ALMOST ANYWHERE**— in a car, in the library, at the park, or in your room—for a few minutes or a few hours. You can embroider while you're listening to music, watching television, or even talking with friends.

The choices are all yours—the stitches, the colors, the threads, the fabrics. Use this book as a guide, but **LET YOUR CREATIVE SIDE LOOSE AND EXPLORE.** Once you learn how to embroider, be sure to teach your friends and even your parents and other relatives.

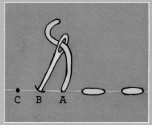

Running stitch, right-handed

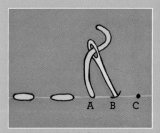

Running stitch, left-handed

# Embroidery Tools

Embroidery is a wonderful craft that you can learn to do with just a few basic tools available at most craft stores. For almost every project, you need fabric, a needle, pins, embroidery scissors, and a short ruler. Ideally, you should keep all of these tools in a special place, such as a basket or small bag. That way you'll never lose your tools, and they'll always be ready and waiting for you when you want to start stitching.

## Embroidery Fabric

Embroidery can be stitched on all sorts of fabric. The type of fabric you choose determines the look of the finished project.

### Fabric for Needlepoint

The two needlepoint projects in this book call for plastic needlepoint canvas. Plastic canvas looks like a giant tic-tac-toe grid. It is very stiff and should be used for projects that do not need to bend. Plastic canvas is usually white and is commonly sold in two counts (7 and 10). This means it has about 7 or 10 boxes per inch. It is the easiest fabric to use when you are learning to needlepoint.

### Fabric for Cross-Stitch

In this book, you cross-stitch on a cheerful checked fabric called gingham. Gingham fabric is great for learning because you can use the checks to make your stitches nice and even.

### Fabric for Free-Form Embroidery

Free-form embroidery can be stitched on just about any fabric, even blue jeans, T-shirts, and sweaters. Many of the projects in this book use wool felt. It is very easy to cut and stitch. Make sure that your needle can easily slip through the fabric you choose. Some fabrics are so

*Continued on page 8*

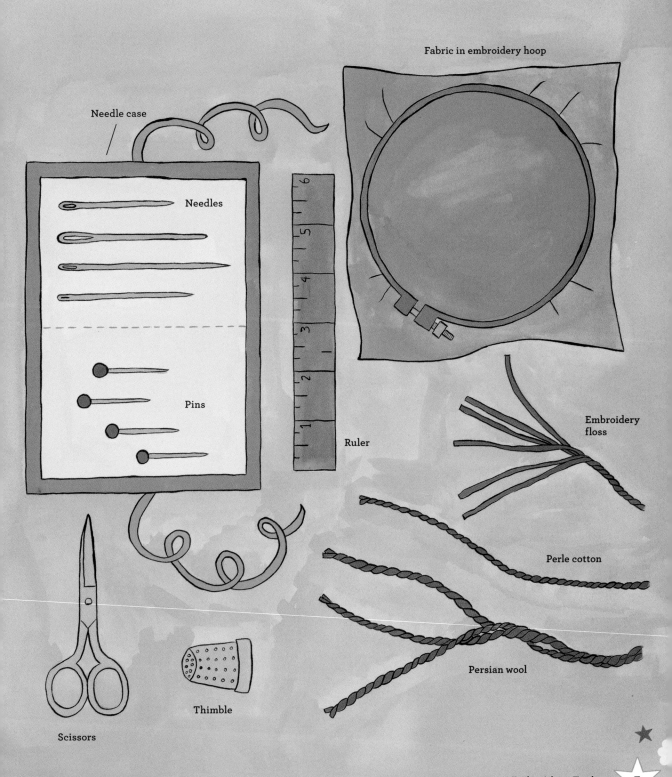

Fabric in embroidery hoop

Needle case

Needles

Pins

Ruler

Embroidery floss

Perle cotton

Persian wool

Scissors

Thimble

tightly woven that it is difficult to sew through them. **IT IS IMPORTANT THAT THE FABRIC IS THICK ENOUGH THAT YOU CAN'T SEE THROUGH IT,** so the knots and threads on the back of the project will not be visible from the front. Natural-fiber fabrics like cotton, wool, and linen are easiest to stitch on. Shop for free-form embroidery fabrics at fabric stores, craft stores, and thrift shops. Or, look in your closets at home for old clothes, sheets, or curtains that you might be able to recycle (with your parents' permission). See Recycling and Reinventing Fabric for Embroidery (page 16) for more ideas.

When you are stitching on fabric that was not specially made for embroidery, it helps to find what is called the straight grain of the fabric (see below).

# STRAIGHT GRAIN OF THE FABRIC

Finding the straight grain of the fabric helps to ensure that your pillow, framed picture, or other projects will look perfect when finished. Straight lines of stitches look better when they follow the straight grain. The edges will be neater and easier to finish if they are straight, instead of wavy with ragged threads.

Woven fabrics are made with two sets of threads that weave over and under each other. One set runs from side to side, from one finished edge to the other, and the other runs up and down from one cut end to the other. In order to trim the edges of your fabric perfectly straight, you need to cut exactly along the line of one of these threads, which is called the straight grain of the fabric.

With gingham, plaid, or striped woven fabrics, it is easy to find the straight grain, because you can see the different colored threads in the fabric running side to side or up and down.

If you pick one thread to follow, such as the edge of a line of checks on gingham, you will be following the straight grain. Cut along that line, and you will be cutting the fabric perfectly straight.

For solid or print fabrics, it can be hard to follow the straight grain along a single thread with your eyes, so you need to follow these steps:

**1 START** with a square or rectangular piece of fabric a few inches bigger all the way around than it needs to be for your project. Pull off the loose threads on 1 edge, fraying the fabric into little fringes. Repeat this step on the other 3 edges of your fabric. Pull away enough threads so that the fabric looks like a solid rectangle or square with threads coming together at a 90° angle in the corners you have frayed.

# Embroidery Thread and Yarn

Embroidery can be done with many different kinds of thread and yarn. Following are descriptions of the most popular choices.

## Cotton

Cotton thread is a good choice for beginners because it glides easily through the fabric. A lot of cotton embroidery thread is prepared by a process called mercerization to make it look shiny like silk. The two most common kinds of cotton thread used for embroidery are embroidery floss and perle cotton.

**2 SELECT** 1 of the horizontal threads about ½˝ below the top thread, and start pulling it out of the fabric to the side. The fabric will begin to pucker. Keep pulling the thread until it is removed, and you will see what looks like a dotted line of holes across the fabric where the thread was. The dotted line is the straight grain of the fabric. If the thread breaks while you are pulling, flatten out the puckered fabric and cut along the dotted line until you reach the point where the thread remains. Then carefully resume pulling the thread.

**3 CUT** along the dotted line to make an edge that is perfectly on the straight grain of the fabric.

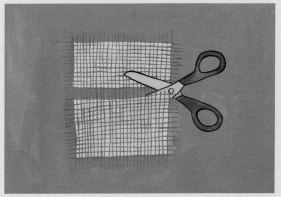

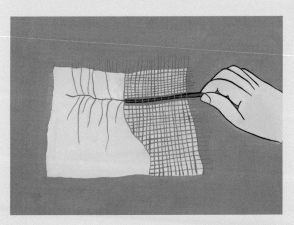

**Embroidery floss:** It is made of six separate strands of cotton thread. It can be used as you purchase it, using all six strands, or separated so you can use two, three, or more strands for stitching (see Separating the Strands, Embroidery Floss and Persian Wool, page 11). Embroidery floss comes in small skeins (rhymes with "lanes") of about 8 yards each and in hundreds of colors.

**Perle cotton:** This is another popular type of thread for embroidery that is shinier than embroidery floss. Three commonly available sizes are #3, #5, and #8. The higher the number, the thinner the thread. Perle cotton covers the base fabric quickly, which makes it a good choice for beginners. It comes in skeins twisted to look like a short rope, and the number of yards varies by size. See Separating the Strands, Perle Cotton (page 12) to learn how to untwist a skein. Perle cotton also comes in small balls, which contain much more thread.

## Wool

Wool yarn is a good choice when you're just learning how to embroider because its slight fuzziness covers the fabric well, and it has a little bit of stretchiness, which can help make slightly uneven stitches look more uniform. Wool is used for needlepoint on canvas, or for free-form embroidery. The most common kind of wool for embroidery is Persian wool.

**Persian wool:** This is made of three separate thinner pieces of yarn that stick loosely together side by side because the wool is slightly fuzzy. Persian wool usually is sold in 30˝ strands or 8-yard skeins. You can purchase it in needlepoint stores. **PERSIAN WOOL IS MADE THIS WAY SO YOU CAN USE IT AS IT COMES,** with all three strands held together, or separated into its individual parts so you can work with one, two, three, or more strands (see Separating the Strands, page 11). The more strands you use, the thicker the stitches.

## Other Threads

Any kind of yarn, thread, or ribbon can be used for embroidery, cross-stitch, or needlepoint as long as it can be threaded through a needle and pulled through the base fabric. If you have a family member who likes to knit or crochet, ask them if you can use their odds and ends of yarn for embroidery. Sometimes embroiderers even use metal threads of silver and gold, silk threads or linen threads to make very fancy fabrics.

### Did You Know?

When embroiderers first began decorating their clothes and household items with stitching, they had to work with threads they spun themselves on hand spindles, or sometimes by just rolling fibers between their hands or along their legs. They colored their threads and fabrics with dyes made from natural materials such as plants, flowers, and even shellfish and bugs.

# Separating the Strands

To keep your threads from becoming tangled, it's important to open the skeins and remove strands in a particular way. Here are instructions for each type of thread used in the projects in this book.

## Embroidery Floss and Persian Wool

Persian wool and embroidery floss each come in a package called a skein with paper bands wrapped around them. The thread is wrapped in a circular formation, and the bands hold the circle tight and neat.

To use these kinds of threads, first you remove a piece from the skein. Then separate it into the number of strands required for your project. (Embroidery floss has 6 strands and Persian wool has 3 strands.)

**TIP**

*Cut your stitching thread short (approximately 20˝) when you are first learning to stitch. Long lengths of thread tangle frequently and will be frustrating. As your skills increase, you can use longer threads. Wool threads will "wear" and become thin because the section of thread close to the needle will go in and out of the fabric more often. Mercerized cotton threads wear too, although not as drastically as wool.*

**1** Find the thread's loose end; it will be sticking out the side of 1 of the loops. Gently pull on the end to release about 30˝ of thread, and then cut off a 20˝ piece.

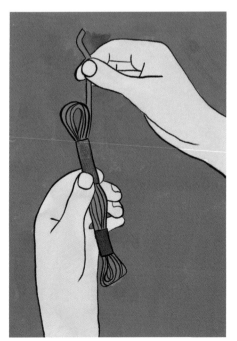

**2** To separate 1 or more strands, hold the 20˝-length in one hand, and with the other hand, fan the cut ends. Gently tug on the number of strands you need for your project to remove them from the bundle. Keep the remaining strands neat and organized so they don't become tangled; you can use them later.

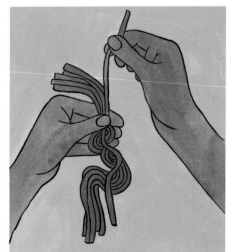

**QUICK TIP**

*When cutting a length of Persian wool or embroidery floss from a skein, be sure to leave about 3˝ of thread sticking out of the skein so that next time you need thread, you will be able to find the end easily.*

## Perle Cotton

To work with perle cotton, first remove the paper bands around the skein.

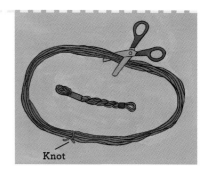

Knot

Carefully open up the skein and untwist so that it looks like a big loop. There will be a knotted tie keeping the threads together. Using scissors, cut through the entire skein at the place opposite the knot. You now have a bundle of pieces of cotton thread about 36˝ long.

To remove 1 strand, hold the bundle near the knot and pull out only 1 strand, leaving the rest of the strands held together with the knotted tie around it.

# Needles

When you visit a craft store, you may be surprised to discover that there are so many different kinds of needles. The directions in this book tell you what kind and size of needle you need for each project. When choosing a needle yourself, remember that it should be slightly thicker than the thread you want to use so it can open a path through the fabric for the thread to follow. When starting out, it is a good idea to buy an assortment pack with many different sizes of the needle types listed. That way, you have a good chance of always having the right needle in your embroidery kit.

## Chenille Needles

Chenille needles are larger than embroidery needles. They have a sharp point and a large oval eye. They are used for many of the free-form embroidery projects in this book. They are very easy to thread and my favorite kind of needle to stitch with.

## Tapestry Needles

Tapestry needles have a rounded, blunt tip with a large eye, which makes them easy to thread. Tapestry needles are usually used for needlepoint.

## Darning Needles

Darning needles are the largest and longest of all the needles. They have a sharp tip and a very large eye. They are commonly used with multiple strands of Persian wool on thick fabric.

## Embroidery Needles

General embroidery needles have a very sharp point that passes through any kind of fabric by piercing it and creating a hole for the thread to pass through. They have long eyes for easy threading. They are commonly used for projects made with cotton embroidery floss.

# Threading a Needle

The techniques shown here will help you to thread your embroidery needle quickly and easily. **BEFORE YOU START, WASH YOUR HANDS SO THEY'RE NOT AT ALL STICKY.** Choose a place to work that is brightly lit. For the projects in this book, you'll generally want to start with a 20˝ length of thread, floss, or yarn. Once you have poked the thread through the eye of the needle, pull at least 6˝ through the needle so that the thread doesn't slip right back out of the eye.

## Simple Threading

For cotton embroidery threads such as floss or perle cotton, or other smooth (nonfuzzy) threads, make a new clean cut at one end of the thread. Moisten the end in your mouth and flatten with your lips as you pull it out. Hold the thread between your thumb and pointer finger with about ¼˝ to ½˝ showing beyond your fingers, and poke it straight through the eye of the needle.

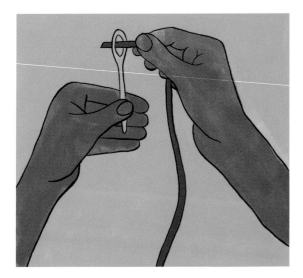

## Loop Method

This method works well with wool or other fuzzy threads that have little hairs on the surface.

**1** Hold your needle between your thumb and finger with about 1˝ of the pointy end of the needle showing. Now fold the end of your thread over the needle with about 1˝ on a side of the needle and the tail dangling on the other side. With the thumb and finger of your other hand, pinch the thread around the needle tightly. Pull the needle out while holding the little loop secure in your other hand.

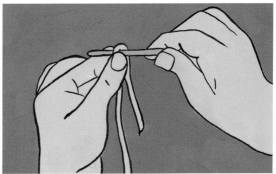

**2** Push the loop through the eye of the needle, and pull the thread through.

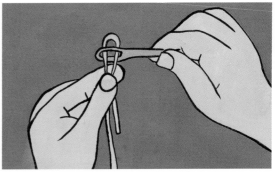

## Using a Needle Threader

To make threading a needle easy, use a needle threader. Push the threader's wire diamond through the eye of the needle first. Poke the end of your thread through the center of the diamond. Pull the needle threader back through the eye, and the thread will follow.

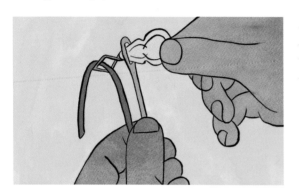

## Using a Double Thread

Some projects require a double strand of thread. Cut a 40˝ length of thread. Thread it through the needle, and pull until the ends meet up. Knot the ends of the 2 strands together. Now 2 strands of thread will be used for stitching.

## Running Out of Thread

As you stitch, when you have about 5˝ or 6˝ of thread left, it's time to secure the thread you're working with and begin a new one. See Ending Stitches and Weaving in the Ends (page 23) for ending your thread on needlepoint and Starting and Stopping (page 34) for ending your thread on cross-stitch and embroidery.

# Other Tools

## Scissors

Ideally, you should have a few different kinds of scissors.

- ✂ **Small scissors with a sharp point** (often called embroidery scissors at the store) for snipping threads and removing mistakes

- ✂ **Large sharp scissors** for cutting fabric and yarn only

- ✂ **Old or very inexpensive scissors** for cutting plastic canvas and paper (sometimes labeled craft or all-purpose scissors)

Label your fabric scissors with a piece of tape or a permanent marker so that you and anyone who might borrow your scissors will remember which ones are for cutting fabric and yarn only. Paper and plastic canvas can dull the blades of your good scissors, making it difficult for them to cut fabric and yarn.

## Pins and Pincushion

The best tool for keeping track of your pins and threaded needles is a pincushion. See Sew Pincushion (page 52) for instructions to make your own. Do not leave needles or pins in your work because they could leave a permanent hole in the fabric, or a rust stain if they got wet. Rust stains are not usually a problem if you buy rustproof pins and needles, but it can happen.

## Needlebook or Magnet

To keep track of your embroidery needles, it's useful to keep them in a small fabric needlebook or on a magnet designed for this purpose. See Needlebook (page 48) for instructions to make your own. You can also keep your needles stuck in a pincushion.

## Embroidery Hoop

Embroidery hoops hold floppy fabric tight and smooth while you are working so your stitches stay even and the fabric does not pucker. They can be used for any cross-stitch or free-form embroidery project as long as the fabric fits between the two halves of the hoop. Some fabrics, such as the wool felt used in many of the projects in this book, do not require an embroidery hoop because they are firm enough on their own.

An embroidery hoop is made of two circles of wood or plastic that fit together with a little space between them for the fabric. They come in different diameters so you can work on different-sized areas of your fabric. WHEN YOU BUY AN EMBROIDERY HOOP, MAKE SURE IT IS SMALLER THAN THE PIECE OF FABRIC YOU WILL BE STITCHING so it can get a good grip on the fabric all around.

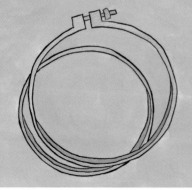

## Ruler and Tape Measure

Ideally, you should have a 6″ ruler, a 12″ ruler, and a tape measure. Clear plastic rulers make it easy to see the fabric or design underneath as you use them. Some clear plastic rulers have graphed lines, which make them very helpful for drawing squares and rectangles and for cutting even pieces of fabric. You can purchase them at art and quilting stores.

## Transfer Tools

For many of the projects in this book, you will need to draw or transfer a design onto your fabric. Depending on the project, you may use an ordinary pencil, an erasable fabric marker, a permanent marker, dressmaker's tracing paper, or computer T-shirt transfers.

Suggestions for which type of transfer tool to use are included in the project instructions. Follow the manufacturer's directions carefully when using any type of erasable transfer tool.

## Masking Tape

Sometimes you will want to tape the edges of your fabric so that it won't unravel while you are working on your project. Fold masking tape (or blue painter's tape) over each edge of the fabric.

If you have a sewing machine, you can zigzag the edges to prevent fraying, instead of using masking tape. You can also use a product such as Fray Check that is applied like glue to the edges of the fabric and allowed to dry.

## Thimble

A thimble looks like a miniature metal cup that you wear on one finger. You can use a thimble to protect the end of your finger when you stitch and to push hard on the needle to move it through thick or tight fabrics like denim. The thimble is covered with little dimples so that the end of the needle doesn't just slip off the thimble while you're pushing the needle. Thimbles can be plain metal or very fancy with decorations and painted designs. Some people like to collect thimbles.

## Needle Threader

There are several different kinds of gadgets available to help you to thread a needle. Most have a thin, flexible wire formed into a diamond shape at one end. See Threading a Needle (pages 13 and 14) to see how a needle threader is used.

## Thread Organizer

Craft and needlework stores carry all kinds of thread organizing systems, or you can create your own system at home. For example, you can use a different plastic zip sandwich bag for each color of thread. Then clip the bags together with a round ring available at office supply stores (similar to a notebook binder ring), and store them in a cardboard box. You can buy plastic boxes for thread storage that come with small pieces of cardboard to wind threads around.

# Recycling and Reinventing Fabric for Embroidery

It's fun and interesting to embroider on fabric that was once used for a different purpose.

## Choosing Fabric to Recycle

Look for fabrics made out of linen, cotton, wool, or silk. Curtains, blankets, bed sheets, wool coats, denim jeans, tablecloths, dish towels, and T-shirts can all be transformed into embroidery fabric.

If you are embroidering on a piece of clothing that you still wear, then you probably don't have to do much to prepare it. Brand-new clothing should be washed according to the instructions on the tag.

When you are recycling a used piece of clothing or a household item, examine it to see where the cleanest and best sections are. **AVOID AREAS OF THE FABRIC THAT ARE WORN, FRAYING, OR STAINED.** Cut out the largest good pieces of fabric, removing any linings, zippers, buttons, and hems, unless you plan on using them as part of your design.

# Dyeing Fabric

If you don't like the color of a piece of fabric, consider dyeing it. **GET AN ADULT'S HELP.** Fabrics made out of natural fibers, such as cotton, wool, rayon, and silk, dye easily. You can purchase fabric dyes at grocery or craft stores. Look for dyes that say on the package that they will work with your kind of fabric. You can dye fabric in a pot in your kitchen or outside, or even in the washing machine.

Follow the directions on the dye package carefully. If you dye white or light-colored fabric, it will turn the color of your dye, but if you dye fabric that's already colored, the starting color of the fabric will affect the results. For example, if you dye yellow fabric with pink dye, the finished fabric will be orange, just as if you were mixing paints.

# Felting Wool Fabric

Wool felt is a fantastic fabric to embroider on—especially when you are just learning to stitch. You can purchase wool felt or make it yourself and save a lot of money.

**FELTING IS A PROCESS OF SHRINKING WOOL FIBERS** to create a thick, soft fabric you can't see through. Most people are familiar with felting by accident, such as when you put a wool sweater in the washing machine and it shrinks down to a size to fit a teddy bear. When you felt fabric on purpose, the results can be wonderful. Felt is an especially good fabric for embroidery and sewing projects because it can be cut into any shape and the edges don't unravel, so you don't need to finish the edges with hems.

To make your own felt, first get your parents' permission and ask them if they want to supervise. **CHOOSE AN OLD WOOL SWEATER, BLANKET, OR COAT** that is at least 80% wool. Make sure it is not a type of wool called superwash, which has been treated with chemicals so that it won't felt. Set the washing machine for a hot water wash and cold rinse; add a little gentle laundry soap (Ivory works well) and a few other clothes that need to be washed (except for bath towels, which may shed). Let the washing machine run on the regular cycle that you use for most clothes (not the wool or delicate cycle). When the cycle is done, remove your fabric from the washing machine and inspect it—it should be thicker and smaller than when it began. **IF YOU WANT IT TO FELT EVEN MORE, RUN IT THROUGH THE WASH CYCLE AGAIN.** When it's ready, spread the felt out flat on towels and leave it to air dry.

# Gridded Stitches

Our embroidery adventure begins with needlepoint and cross-stitch—two easy stitches sewn in a squared or gridded fashion. Needlepoint is stitched on an open-weave fabric. Needlepoint stitches cover the surface of the grid, actually making a new surface. Cross-stitch is made with two diagonal stitches forming an X.

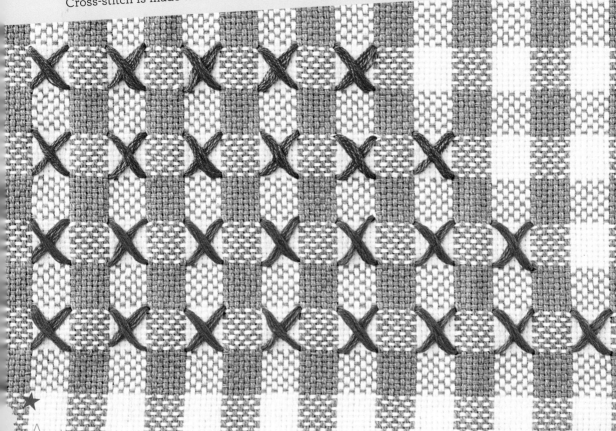

# Needlepoint

When you needlepoint, you cover the entire front of a canvas fabric with stitches—none of the fabric underneath will show through. Traditionally, needlepoint is stitched with wool yarn because it covers the fabric easily. Needlepoint is usually done on a specially treated, stiff fabric called needlepoint mesh, or on plastic canvas. The needlepoint projects in this book use plastic canvas.

Sometimes the needlepoint design is printed directly on the mesh or canvas for you to stitch like paint-by-number, and other times you need to follow a separate chart. Of course, you can make up your own designs, too.

# Tent Stitch

Tent stitch is the easiest stitch in needlepoint and is used for both projects in this chapter.

**1** Thread your needle and come up at A (see the illustration at right). Pull the thread through, leaving a tail of about 6˝ on the back.

**2** Hold this tail against the back of the canvas as you take the first 3 or 4 stitches so it doesn't pull right through. After you have made a few stitches, it will be secure.

**3** Move your needle over and up 1 space, and then insert it at B. Pull through to the back of the canvas, making a short diagonal stitch that covers 1 intersection of the canvas.

**4** Bring the needle to the front 1 space below B at C, and pull to the front.

**5** Count over 1 space and up 1 space again. Insert the needle at D, and pull the thread through to form the second diagonal stitch in the row. Continue across the row, ending at J, the end of your first row of stitches.

**6** Leave the thread at the back after the last stitch, and **rotate the plastic canvas so the first row of stitches is now at the top.**

## ROW 2 AND SO FORTH:

**1** Insert your needle at K—in the first row of holes below where you left the thread at the end of the previous row. Pull the thread through to the front of the canvas.

**2** Count over and up 1 space again, and insert the needle at L, in the same hole as a stitch from the previous row. Pull the thread through to the back to form the first diagonal stitch in this row.

**3** Bring the needle to the front 1 space below L at M, and pull to the front. Count over and up 1 space again, and insert the needle at N to form the second diagonal stitch in the row.

**4** Continue across the row in this way until you have completed the second row of stitches.

**5** At the end of the row of stitches, leave the thread at the back of the work, and rotate your plastic canvas again for the third row of stitching. Insert the needle 1 space above where you left the thread at the end of the previous row. Pull the thread through to the front, and stitch the third row just like the first row.

## Note

As long as you rotate your plastic canvas at the end of each row, you can continue to make all the rows of stitches in the same direction.

### TIP

*When you needlepoint, it is very important that all of your stitches lean in the same direction so they fit snugly together side by side and cover the canvas completely. If the stitches lean in different directions, the plastic canvas (or fabric) may show through where the stitches don't touch each other, and your work will not appear even and neat. When you are learning, it is easier to make sure all the stitches are leaning in the same direction if you stitch in a very orderly manner from one side of the canvas to the other.*

# Edge Stitch

Trim your canvas so that here is 1 intersection of plastic all around the stitching. Cut 2 pieces of thread 32″ long. Hold both pieces together and thread them on the needle. You will be working the edging with 2 strands.

To begin edge stitching, bring the thread up to the front through one of the holes in the middle of the line of holes. Pull the thread through, leaving a tail about 6″ long on the back of the work to weave in later. Hold this tail against the back of the canvas as you take the first 3 or 4 stiches or else it will pull right through!

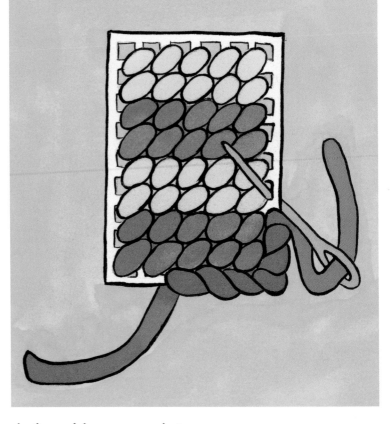

Edge stitch all the way around the project as shown (at right). Bring the needle from the back to the front of the canvas each time, moving over one hole with each stitch. Each stitch will wrap around the edge of the canvas slant to cover the edge of the canvas. At each corner, make 2 stitches into the same hole so the plastic doesn't show. Finish by turning the work to the wrong side and weaving the tail behind the other stitches (see Ending Stitches and Weaving in the Ends, page 23).

# ENDING STITCHES AND WEAVING IN THE ENDS

When you are finished stitching or have less than 5˝ of thread left, bring the thread to the back of the canvas. Secure the end by weaving it under the stitches on the back of the fabric for about ½˝, as shown. Trim the end of the tail to ¼˝ long.

To finish the tail from where you began stitching, thread the tail on a needle. Weave it under the stitches on the back for about ½˝. Trim the end of the tail to ¼˝ long.

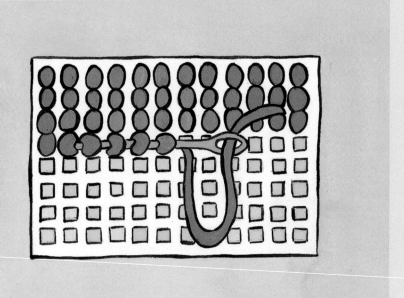

Weave thread tail on back of canvas.

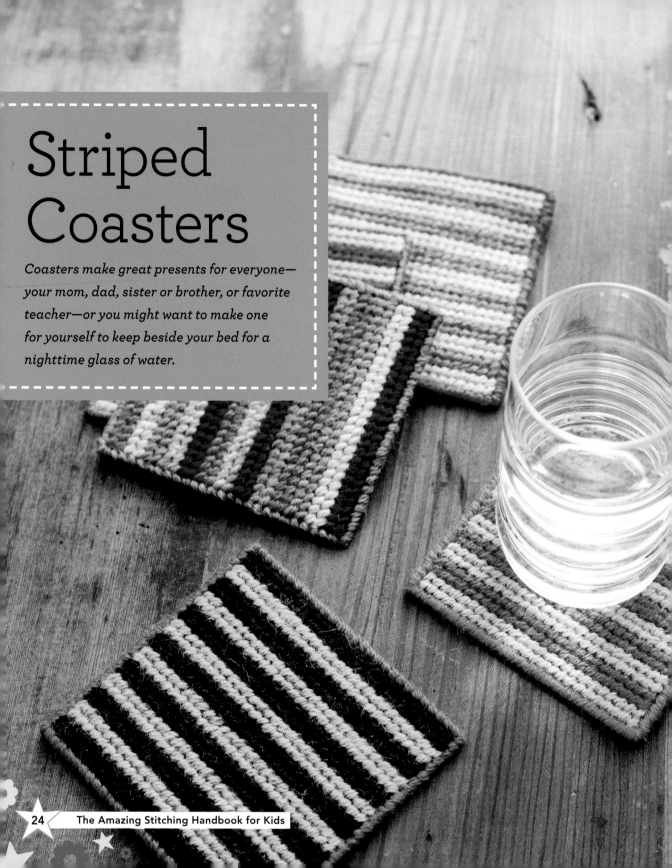

# Striped Coasters

*Coasters make great presents for everyone—your mom, dad, sister or brother, or favorite teacher—or you might want to make one for yourself to keep beside your bed for a nighttime glass of water.*

# Set Up

**1** For each coaster, use your craft scissors to cut a piece of plastic canvas about 5˝ square (see Cutting Plastic Canvas, page 27). Make sure to trim the nibs all the way around so that your thread won't catch on them. This is a bigger area than you will need for stitching; you will trim the extra canvas close to your stitching when you are finished.

**2** For this project, you need to thread your needle with 2 strands of worsted yarn. Cut 2 strands of yarn 20˝ long, and thread both pieces onto the needle.

# Stitch It

## Stripe 1:

**1** Using the threaded needle, bring the yarn up to the front through the hole in the lower left corner of the canvas. Pull the yarn through, leaving a 6˝ long tail on the back to weave in later.

**2** Hold the tail against the back of the canvas as you take the first 3 or 4 stitches so it doesn't pull right through. After you have made a few stitches, the yarn will be anchored securely.

**3** Sew 25 *tent stitches* across from left to right. When you get to the end of the row, there will be some leftover canvas beyond it. Just leave this part empty; you will trim it away when you get ready to finish the coaster.

**4** Rotate your canvas so the first row of stitches is at the top. Sew another row of 25 tent stitches to make the second row of your stripe.

**5** Finish off this color of yarn on the back of the canvas after the last stitch (see Ending Stitches and Weaving in the Ends, page 23).

## Stitches used:
tent stitch (page 20)
edge stitch (page 22)

## Materials
*Makes 4 coasters.*

- 1 piece plastic needlepoint canvas in 7 mesh size, 10½˝ × 13½˝
- Worsted wool yarn scraps in 3–6 colors*
- Tapestry needle, size 16
- Craft scissors, for cutting plastic canvas
- Sharp scissors for cutting yarn
- 4 felt pieces, 4½˝ × 4½˝ (*optional*)
- Fabric glue to attach felt (*optional*)

*\* For each coaster, you will need 3 to 6 colors of worsted yarn. Worsted yarn is often used for knitting and is the perfect yarn for stitching needlepoint. Ask family friends who knit or crochet if they have any to give you. They will be happy to give you their scraps.*

## Stripe 2:

**1** Thread 2 strands of the new color on the needle. Turn the canvas so the first stripe is at the bottom. Bring the needle up to the front

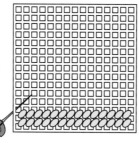

through the hole on the left side of the canvas, directly above the second row of the first stripe.

**2** Stitch 2 rows for the second stripe and finish off the yarn the same way you did with the first stripe (see Stripe 1, page 25).

**3** Continue to stitch 2 rows for each stripe, alternating colors until your coaster looks like the photo (below). You will have 13 stripes in all—7 of the first color and 6 of the second color.

**Finished 2-color coaster**

## Multicolor Coaster Option:

To make the multicolor stripe coaster, stitch the stripes in the following order:

**stripe 1**—pink            **stripe 8**—red

**stripe 2**—light green     **stripe 9**—chartreuse

**stripe 3**—aqua           **stripe 10**—pink

**stripe 4**—gold           **stripe 11**—aqua

**stripe 5**—red            **stripe 12**—light green

**stripe 6**—pink           **stripe 13**—red.

**stripe 7**—gold

Feel free to make up your own combination of stripes.

**Finished multicolor coaster**

# Finish It

**1** Trim your canvas so there is 1 intersection of plastic all around the stitching.

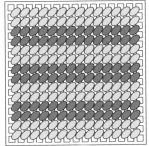

**2** Thread 2 strands of your third color yarn on your needle. Bring the yarn up to the front through 1 of the holes in the middle of the line of holes across the bottom of the coaster. Pull the yarn through. Leave a tail of about 6˝ at the back.

**3** Hold the tail against the back of the canvas as you take the first 3 or 4 stitches so it doesn't pull right through. Sew an **edge stitch** all the way around the coaster. At each corner, take 2 stitches into the same hole so the plastic doesn't show.

**4** Finish with the thread on the back of the canvas after the last stitch. Secure the end of the thread (see Ending Stitches and Weaving the Ends, page 23). Secure the beginning tail in the same way.

## Felt Backing (*optional*)

A felt backing is a nice way to finish the back of your coasters.

**1** Place the coaster on a piece of felt, and trace all the way around the coaster.

**2** Using fabric scissors, cut out the felt just inside the traced line. The felt should be a little smaller than the coaster so it does not show from the front.

**3** Following the directions on the fabric glue package, carefully glue the felt to the back of the coaster. Let it dry.

# CUTTING PLASTIC CANVAS

**1** **DRAW** the shape of your project on the plastic canvas using a removable marker.

**2** **USING** craft scissors (not the scissors you use to cut fabric or your embroidery scissors), cut the canvas about an inch or more outside the line. Cut 1 strand of plastic at a time. Each strand will "pop" as you cut it.

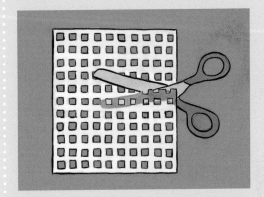

**Note:** *Cutting the canvas bigger than the actual project makes it easier to hold the canvas when stitching close to the edge. When you are finished, you can cut away the extra canvas according to the directions for your project.*

**3** **AFTER** cutting your shape, snip off the little nibs (points) around the edge of the canvas so that your thread will not catch on them while stitching.

**4** **FOLLOW** the marker manufacturer's directions to remove the marker lines before stitching.

# Stitch-It Photo Frame

*Do you have a favorite pet that you want to frame a photo of for your room? Or, maybe you'd like to frame your school picture for your grandparents for a gift. This photo frame is something everyone will like, and they will remember you every time they look at it. To make it into a magnet for a refrigerator, glue magnets on the back.*

# Set Up

**1** Cut a piece of plastic canvas 7½″ × 9″ (see Cutting Plastic Canvas, page 27). Trim the plastic nibs all the way around so that your yarn won't catch on them.

**2** Cut 20″ of wool yarn and then thread your needle with 2 strands. Use the color you want for the outer part of the frame.

## Stitches used:

tent stitch (page 20)
edge stitch (page 22)

## Materials

*Makes 1 frame for a 5″ × 7″ photo.*

- • • 8″ × 10″ plastic needlepoint canvas in 7 mesh size

- • • Worsted wool yarn* in 3 colors

- • • Size 16 tapestry needle

- • • Craft scissors, for cutting plastic canvas and cardboard

- • • Fabric scissors

- • • Piece of cardboard for covering back of frame

- • • Pencil

- • • Craft glue, to attach cardboard to back of frame

- • • 5″ × 7″ photo

*\* To make this photo frame, you will need 3 colors of worsted knitting yarn. It comes in acrylic and wool. As a beginner, it is best to use pure wool yarn. It is easier to stitch with and is more forgiving than acrylic yarn.*

# Stitch It

## Outside Stripe

**1** Bring the yarn up to the front through the hole in the lower left corner of the canvas.

**2** Pull the yarn through, leaving a tail about 6″ long on the back of the canvas to weave in later. Hold this tail against the back of the canvas as you take the first 3 or 4 stitches, so it doesn't pull right through.

**3** Sew 44 *tent stitches* from left to right to complete the row.

**4** Rotate your canvas so the first row of stitches is at the top, and sew another row of stitches to make the second row.

**5** Finish off this color of yarn on the back of the canvas after the last stitch. Weave it behind the other stitches for about ½″ (see Ending Stitches and Weaving in the Ends, page 23). Secure the beginning tail as well.

**6** Repeat Steps 1–5 at each of the 3 remaining sides, using the same yarn color. Sew 2 rows of 58 tent stitches on the left and right sides of the frame. Then sew 2 rows of 44 stitches on the top.

## Middle Stripe

**1** Thread 2 strands of your second color yarn on the needle.

**2** Bring the thread up to the front through the hole on the next empty row, directly above the second row of stitches. Stitch the middle stripe the same as the first stripe covering 4 rows of canvas.

## Inner Stripe

Using the third yarn, sew 1 row of tent stitches all the way around the frame, just inside the middle stripe.

**The Amazing Stitching Handbook for Kids**

# Finish It

**1** Trim away the excess plastic canvas along the outside of the stitched frame, leaving 1 row of plastic.

**2** Make the frame edge using an *edge stitch*. Use 2 strands of yarn in the same color as the outer stripe. Begin by bringing the yarn up to the front through 1 of the holes in the middle of 1 edge.

**3** Pull the thread through, leaving a tail about 6˝ long on the back of the canvas to weave in later. Hold this tail against the back of the canvas as you take the first 3 or 4 stitches so it doesn't pull right through. Edgestitch all the way around the frame.

**4** At each corner, you will need to take 2 stitches into the same hole so the plastic doesn't show.

**5** When you have gone all the way around the coaster, finish by leaving the yarn on the back (see Ending Stitches and Weaving the Ends, page 23). Secure the beginning tail in the same way.

**6** Using sharp scissors, cut out the center of the canvas, making a space for your photo. Leave a row of plastic at the inside of the frame to sew the inner row of whipstitch on.

**7** Sew the inner edge in whipstitch as you did on your outer edge (Steps 1–5, above).

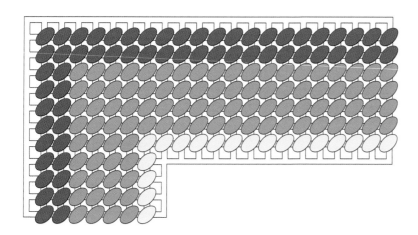

**8** To create the cardboard backing, place the frame on a piece of cardboard. Trace around the frame using a pencil. Using craft scissors, cut out the backing piece, just inside the drawn line.

**9** Run a thin line of glue on the back of the needlepoint frame ¼˝ in from outer edge along the 2 long sides and 1 short side. The side without glue is where you will slip your picture in, so keep it neat and glue-free.

**10** Apply the cardboard to the back of the frame. Weight the frame down with a heavy book. Let the glue dry completely.

# Cross-Stitch

Cross-stitch is similar to needlepoint but instead of making a single diagonal stitch, you make two stitches that cross to form an X. It is sewn on fabric that has a squared design woven in. It is easy to learn cross-stitch on checked fabric like gingham. The checks are large and make a good guide for your X's.

## Did You Know?

In colonial days, young girls were taught to do cross-stitch at home or at school around the same time they were taught to read and write. They often learned the alphabet by sewing it in cross-stitch.

**TIP**

*If you like cross-stitch, you can learn counted cross-stitch. Counted cross-stitch is sewn on a soft, solid-colored fabric called Aida cloth. The stitcher follows the colors on a graphed chart to create the pattern.*

## Cross-Stitch on Gingham

**1** Thread your needle and make a double knot in the end of the thread (see Starting and Stopping, page 34). Bring the needle from the back to the front of the fabric (A), in the lower left corner of a white square. Pull the thread through.

**2** Insert the needle at the upper right corner of the same white check (B), and pull the thread through to the back.

**3** Bring the needle back to the front of the fabric (C), at the bottom left corner of the next white square to the right, and pull the thread to the front.

**4** Continue stitching like this from left to right until the row is finished. The stitching will look like a line of diagonal stitches 1 square apart.

**5** Bring the needle to the front in the lower right corner of the same white check where you stopped (D).

**6** Insert the needle into the upper left corner of the same white check (E), and pull the thread to the back of the fabric to complete 1 cross.

**7** Continue working from right to left across the row to complete all the X's.

**8** To end the stitching, leave the thread on the back of the fabric after crossing the last stitch. Make a stitched knot right behind the last stitch.

# STARTING AND STOPPING

To make sure your embroidery stitches don't come undone, it's important to start and end the embroidery thread properly. For the cross-stitch and freeform embroidery projects in this book, you start with a double knot and end with a stitched knot.

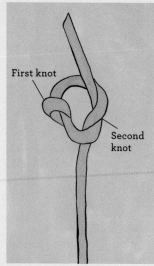

First knot

Second knot

Starting with a double knot

Stopping with a stitched knot on the back of the project

## Double Knot

To start with a double knot, after threading your needle, make 2 knots on top of each other at the end of your thread, then trim the tail to about ¼˝. To begin embroidering, place the needle under the fabric, and poke it through to the front side where you want to begin. Pull the threaded needle through until the knot catches on the back of the fabric.

## Stitched Knot

When you are finished with a piece of thread (or want to change colors), bring the thread to the back of your project. Behind the last stitch, make 3 tiny, tight stitches on top of each other. Make each stitch at a right angle to the 1 before. Trim the end of the thread to about ¼˝.

## Weaving the Ends

Another way to finish a thread is to weave it under the threads on the back of the fabric. Then clip the thread, leaving a ¼˝ tail.

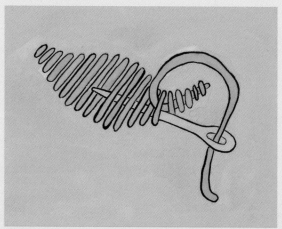

Weave thread in and out of the running stitches on back side of fabric to secure.

Weave thread under satin stitches on back side of fabric to secure.

# Cross-Stitch Dish Towels

*Gingham fabric, sometimes called checked fabric, is very cheerful. It has been popular for hundreds of years. It is very often used in kitchens and interiors, but you may have a summer shirt or skirt made out of it. Once you learn how to make these dish towels, you can look for other gingham fabric items—table runners, place mats, pillowcases, dresses, and shirts—and decorate them with cross-stitch.*

*You may want to use an embroidery hoop when you are cross-stitching on gingham. An embroidery hoop (page 15) makes it easier to embroider on the fabric and to keep the stitches even.*

## Stitches used:

cross-stitch (page 33)

## Materials

*Makes 1 dish towel.*

- 1 gingham-checked cotton dish towel— available at kitchen stores
- 1 skein embroidery floss, in a color darker than the darkest color in your dish towel
- Sharp-pointed embroidery or chenille needle
- Embroidery scissors
- Ruler
- Erasable fabric marker in a color that will show on your fabric
- 6˝ embroidery hoop (*optional*)
- Thick towel for blocking
- Steam iron

# Set Up

**1** Decide if you want to work with all 6 strands of embroidery floss, the way it comes in the package, or divide it (see Separating Strands, page 11) and work with fewer strands. The more strands you use, the darker your X's will be.

**2** Mark your embroidery space using an erasable fabric marker. Draw a line about 2˝ up from the bottom of 1 narrow end of the dish towel along a row of white squares. Draw another line 4 rows of white squares above your first line. For this project, you will be stitching an X in the white boxes, making 4 rows of X's all the way across the towel.

# Stitch It

**1** If you would like, place the marked area of the dish towel in an embroidery hoop (see Using an Embroidery Hoop, page 37). The entire cloth won't fit into the space of the hoop, so place the fabric in the hoop so you can begin at 1 corner of the fabric, and move the hoop as you complete each section.

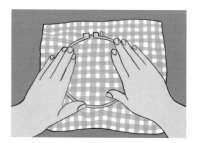

**2** Thread your needle and make a double knot in the end of the thread (page 34). Start with a row of white boxes. Bring the thread to the front of the fabric at the lower left corner of a white square, and sew in *cross-stitch*. Stitch in every white square of the 4 rows within your marked embroidery space. Take care to cross your stitches in the same direction each time so they will appear neat and uniform.

**3** To end the stitching, leave the thread on the back of the fabric after crossing the last stitch. Turn the project over, and make a stitched knot (see Starting and Stopping, page 34). If you run out of thread or need to start a new thread, start and end the thread in the same way.

# Finish It

**1** Remove the erasable marker lines following the manufacturer's directions.

**2** Block the towel (see Blocking to Finish, page 59). Lay the dish towel facedown on a bath towel, and iron it with a steam iron to even out the stitches.

### TIP

*You could fancy up any towel with cross-stitches or other stitches in the book. They would make great personalized gifts.*

### Did You Know?

The name gingham comes from a Dutch word, *gingang*, which is how the seventeenth-century Dutch traders pronounced a Malaysian word for striped cloth.

# USING AN EMBROIDERY HOOP

To place fabric in an embroidery hoop, undo the screw that holds the 2 pieces of the hoop together. Put the smaller half of the hoop (without the screw) on a table. Lay the fabric on top, with the area you will stitch in the center of the hoop. Push the larger half of the hoop (with the screw) down over the lower hoop and fabric. Tighten the screw a little bit, so the fabric does not slide easily between the 2 hoops. Gently tug on the edges of the fabric to make the center of the circle smooth and stretched tight. Then turn the screw the rest of the way so the fabric doesn't move between the hoops. When you finish embroidering the section in the hoop, remove the hoop by loosening the screw. Move the hoop to the next section you want to stitch.

When you finish stitching for the day, always remove your fabric from the hoop. If you don't remove it, the hoop may create a permanent round wrinkle in the fabric.

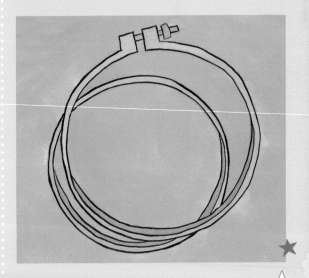

# Basic Free-Form Embroidery

Up to this point, you've been embroidering single stitches for needlepoint and X's for cross-stitch on a grid. With basic free-form stitches, you have a lot more choices. In fact, you can embroider on just about any fabric in any direction. Doing free-form embroidery is like drawing with thread. Think of the fabric as your paper and the thread as your pencils or markers.

The projects in this chapter use 7 basic free-form embroidery stitches. All of these stitches are called straight stitches because by themselves they look like straight lines of different lengths.

# Learning Free-Form Embroidery

To learn the basic free-form embroidery stitches, either dive right into the projects in this chapter and learn as you go, or practice each stitch first on a piece of plain, solid-color cotton scrap fabric using a 6-strand length of embroidery floss about 20˝ long and a large-eyed, sharp-pointed embroidery or chenille needle.

## Two Stitching Methods

Most embroidery stitches can be formed in two steps or in a one-step scooping motion. Often it is easier to learn a stitch as a two-step process; then, once you get the hang of it, you can easily switch to the faster scoop style.

### TWO-STEP METHOD

Secure the thread with a double knot (page 34). Bring the needle to the front side of the fabric from the back, and pull the thread through to the front. Make sure you don't leave any thread on the back. For the first step, insert the needle, send it back to the underside of the fabric, and pull the thread through to the back. For the second step, push the needle from the back to the front and pull it through.

### SCOOP METHOD

Secure the thread with a double knot. Bring the needle from the back to the front where you want your first stitch. All in one motion, insert the needle in the fabric from front to back, and bring it back out on the front again (like scooping a shovel full of sand from the beach), then pull up the thread.

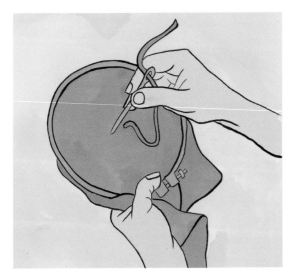

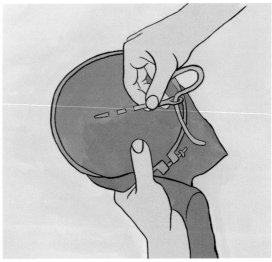

# Running Stitch

A running stitch looks like the dashed line in the middle of a road. It is good for outlining shapes and for making decorative borders. It can also be used to sew together pieces of fabric.

Draw a straight or curvy line on a scrap of fabric. Your stitches will follow this line. Running stitches can be long or short—it's up to you—but they will look better if they are all about the same size.

## Two-Step Method

**1** Secure your thread on the back of the fabric with a double knot (page 34), and bring your needle to the front at A. Pull all the thread through to the front of the fabric. Insert your needle at B, and pull your thread all the way through to the back of the project.

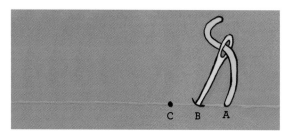

**2** Bring your needle up again at C, and pull the thread all the way through to the front side.

**3** Repeat until you have stitched the entire practice line.

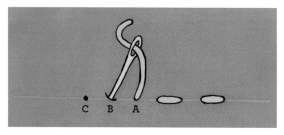

## Scoop Method

**1** Secure your thread on the back of the fabric with a double knot, and come up at A. Pull the thread through to the front.

**2** Insert your needle at B, then scoop the fabric with the tip of your needle, and come up at C in 1 motion. Pull the needle until the thread tightens.

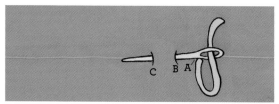

**Note:** If the fabric puckers, you are pulling too tightly. Slip the point of your needle under the thread, and loosen the stitch you just made so it lies flat.

**3** Continue to stitch, following your practice line. Eventually, you will be able to take several stitches at a time before pulling the thread through.

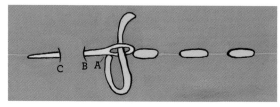

## Finish

For either method, when you finish stitching, secure the thread on the back and weave it under the stitches (see Starting and Stopping, page 34).

# Seed Stitch

The seed stitch is a group of tiny stitches randomly placed close together to create an interesting texture. It can be used to fill shapes or to create a spotted surface.

Secure your thread on the back of the fabric with a double knot (page 34). Bring the needle and thread to the front (A). Pull the thread through.

## Two-Step Method

Insert your needle in the fabric (B), and pull your thread all the way through to the back of the work. Bring your needle up again (C), and pull the thread all the way through to the front side.

## Scoop Method

Once you've practiced a little, you can sew seed stitches in 1 step. After you have pushed the needle down (B), scoop the fabric with the tip of your needle, and come up (C) in 1 motion. Pull the needle until the thread tightens. Continue making the stitches at random, changing the direction of the stitches to look like scattered seeds.

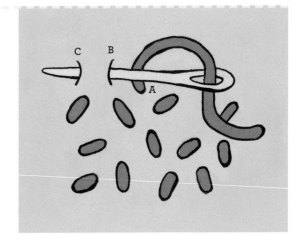

Finish by taking the thread to the back and weaving it under the stitches.

# Backstitch

Backstitch is best sewn using the scoop method. It is like a dance where you go one step back, then two steps forward. Backstitch makes a nice outline for curvy shapes and for stitching letters and words. It can also be used to sew together two pieces of fabric because it is very strong.

To practice, draw a circle on a scrap of cloth.

**1** Secure your thread on the back of the fabric with a double knot (page 34). Bring the needle and thread to the front (A).

**2** Insert your needle into the fabric (B) behind the point where your thread comes out of the fabric, then scoop the needle back to the front of the fabric (C) ahead of your starting point with a single scooping motion. Pull the thread through.

**3** Insert the needle (A) and scoop it to the front (D). Continue around the circle.

**4** On the last stitch that closes the circle, finish by taking the thread to the back and weaving it under the stitches (see Starting and Stopping, page 34).

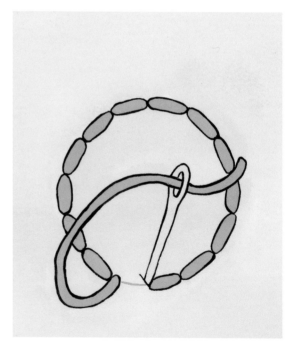

# Stem Stitch

A stem stitch (sometimes called "outline stitch") uses the scoop method. It is good for straight and curvy lines and looks a little thicker than backstitch. It is fun to stitch your name in stem stitch.

**1** Secure your thread on the back of the fabric with a double knot (page 34). Bring the needle to the front (A), and pull the thread through.

**2** Working from right to left in a scooping motion, insert your needle into the fabric (B), and come back up (C) halfway between A and B. Hold the thread down with your finger or thumb so it lies to 1 side of the needle. Pull the thread through.

**3** Holding the thread on the same side of the needle again, insert the needle in the fabric (D), and bring it back to the front in the same hole at B. Pull through and continue.

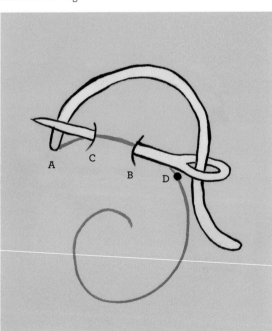

### TIP

*Always hold the thread to the same side of the needle as you work, either on the top or on the bottom. If you don't, your outline will look jagged instead of smooth. Try to make all the stitches the same size. When working around a curve, place your stitches very close together.*

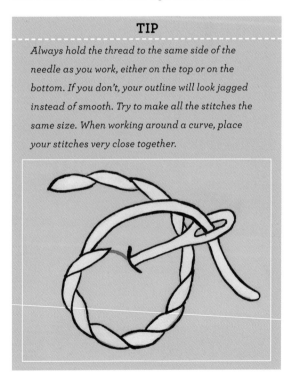

**4** Repeat Step 3 until you reach the end of your curvy line. Finish by taking the thread to the back and weaving it under the stitches (see Starting and Stopping, page 34).

# Satin Stitch

**A SATIN STITCH IS SOMETIMES CALLED A FILLING STITCH** because it is used to fill in large spaces and to make solid shapes. The stitches are sewn very closely together. You can sew satin stitches all the same length to fill straight-edged shapes like squares, or use different length stitches—straight or on a slant—to fill circle, leaf, or flower shapes. It's easiest to learn satin stitch using the two-step method, but after you've gotten the hang of it, you'll probably want to use the scoop method.

Secure your thread on the back of the fabric with a double knot (page 34), and bring it to the front (A). Pull the thread through.

## Two-Step Method

**1** Insert the needle into the fabric (B), and pull the thread through to the back.

**2** Come up to the front (C) right next to the beginning of your first stitch (A), and pull the thread to the front. Then insert the needle (D) right next to the end of your first stitch (B), and pull the thread through to the back.

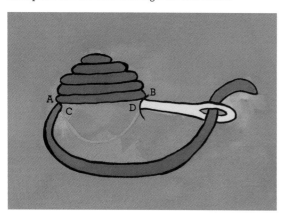

## Scoop Method

Insert the needle into the back of the fabric (B) and bring it to the front (C) in 1 scooping motion. If a stitch is too tight, slip the point of the needle under the stitch and loosen it so it lies flat.

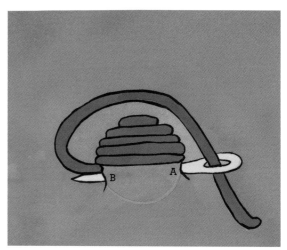

## Finish

For both methods, take the thread to the back and weave it under the stitches (see Weaving the Ends, page 34).

# Straight Stitch

The straight stitch can be used to form flowers, trees, bicycle wheels, sunrays, or any other shape you want. This example shows a seven-pointed star.

**1** To make a star, begin by drawing a circle on your fabric by tracing around a coin with an erasable fabric marker. Make 7 dots around the circle.

**2** Secure your thread on the back of the fabric with a double knot (page 34), and bring it to the front at the center of the circle (A). Pull the thread through. Insert the needle into the fabric on the circle (B), and pull the thread through to the back.

**3** Bring the needle back to the front again at A, and insert it on the circle (C), a short distance from B.

**4** Continue around the circle until you have filled it with 7 spokes. If your stitching is too tight, slip the point of your needle under the thread, and loosen the stitch you just made so it lies flat.

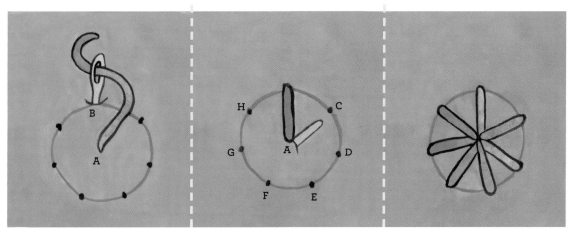

**5** Finish by taking the thread to the back and weaving it under the stitches (see Weaving the Ends, page 34).

You can build many shapes with straight stitches. Experiment on your own to see what you can create.

# Whipstitch

A WHIPSTITCH CAN BE VERY DECORATIVE, OR IT CAN BE USED TO CLOSE THE OPENING OF A PILLOW OR STUFFED TOY. For a decorative whipstitch, use floss. When closing an opening, use sewing thread.

**1** Secure your thread on the back of the fabric with a double knot (page 34) and come up at A. Pull the thread through.

**2** Hold the fabric with the edge you are enclosing nearest to you. Pull the needle toward you, and tuck it under the fabric. Then poke it up through the fabric from back to front at B.

**3** Pull the thread through to the front side of the fabric. A diagonal line will form. Repeat however many times you like. The thread should lie flat. If your stitching is too tight, slip the point of your needle under the thread and loosen it.

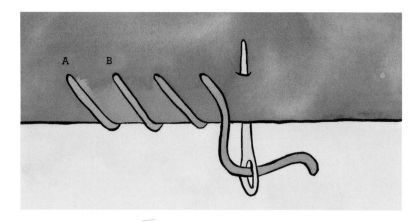

Finish by taking the thread to the back and weaving it under the stitches (see Weaving the Ends, page 34).

## SPACING STITCHES EVENLY

*Sewing a whipstitch on fabric takes a little practice, and can be easier if you mark all your stitching holes first. Use a ruler or tape measure to keep the marks even. Place a small dot using an erasable fabric marker at each stitch point. Make sure the marks are all the same distance from the edge of the fabric, and all the same distance apart from each other.*

# TRANSFERRING DESIGNS TO FABRIC

Before you begin stitching, you may want to transfer a design to your fabric. For the projects in this book, you can use the Window Tracing Method or the Dressmaker's Tracing Paper Method.

For either method, begin by making a photocopy of the design, increasing it in size if needed, or trace it on a piece of paper. Cut around the outside of the design, leaving a ¼˝ border of blank paper all around. The border makes it easier to handle the design and place it where you want it on your fabric.

## Window Tracing Method

Tape the copy to a sunny window, and then tape the fabric on top of the copy so the sun shines through both the paper and the fabric. Make sure the design is positioned where you want it on your fabric, moving the fabric around if necessary.

With an erasable marker (if you need to remove the marks later), a pencil, or a permanent marker (if you will be covering the marks completely), trace the design onto the fabric. Use a color of marker or pencil that will show on your fabric. You can also use a sharp-pointed piece of chalk for tracing and then carefully brush away all traces of the chalk when you have finished stitching.

## Dressmaker's Tracing Paper Method

This method uses dressmaker's tracing paper, which is available at fabric, quilting, and craft stores. Each package usually includes several different colors. Choose a color that will show up well on your embroidery fabric. For instance, if your fabric is dark blue, use white tracing paper. This method is great for transferring designs to felt.

**1 LAY** your fabric on a hard, flat surface, and place the tracing paper on top of the fabric with the waxy side down.

**2 THEN** place your paper design on top of the tracing paper. Make sure the design is positioned where you want it on your fabric. Pin all 3 layers (fabric, tracing paper, and design paper) together so they don't shift.

**3 USING** a ballpoint pen, trace right on top of the lines of the design, pressing firmly. When you are finished, the design will be on the fabric.

# Needlebook

*Needlebooks are fun first stitching projects. They are quick to stitch. When you finish, you can place all your embroidery needles in the book and carry them with you. If you keep stitching for years, you'll have this project to use as a reminder of your first project. Homemade wool felt works nicely (see Felting Wool Fabric, page 17).*

# Set Up

**1** Felt color 1 (book cover and pockets):

Cut 1 piece 3½″ × 5½″ for the cover.

Cut 2 pieces 2½″ × 3½″ each for the pockets.

**2** Felt color 2 (pages):

Cut 2 pieces 5″ × 3″ for the pages.

# Stitch It

**1** Pin a pocket to each end of the cover, matching the edges. Leave a gap ½″ wide in the center.

**2** Thread the needle with a 20″ piece of embroidery floss, and tie a double knot in the end. Hide the starting knot (see Hiding a Knot or an End, page 51).

**3** Sew a **running stitch** around the outer edges, stitching through both layers. Try your best to make each stitch about ¼″ long.

**4** Finish by making a stitched knot (page 34) in between the 2 layers. Trim the end of the thread very close to the felt so it won't stick out.

**5** Place the 2 inside pages exactly on top of each other.

## Materials

*Makes 1 needlebook.*

- Wool felt in 2 colors
- 1 skein of cotton embroidery floss
- Chenille needle
- Fabric scissors
- Embroidery scissors
- Ruler
- Erasable fabric marker
- Pins
- ½ yard grosgrain ribbon, ¼″ wide
- Fabric glue

**6** With the cover pocket side up, place the pages on top of the cover, matching the center of the

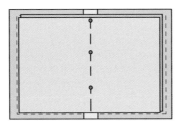

pages with the gap in the center of the cover. Pin them to the cover.

**7** Thread the needle with a new length of floss, and make a double knot in the end. To hide the starting knot, insert the needle between the 2 layers of felt at the midpoint of the lower edge, about ¼˝ from the edge, between the outer page and the cover. Sew running stitches approximately ¼˝ long and ¼˝ apart, through all 3 layers down the center of the cover.

Stitch through all layers.

**8** Finish by bringing your floss to the inside between the cover and outer page. Make a stitched knot (page 34), and trim the floss very close to the felt so it won't stick out. Fold the needlebook closed like a book.

# Finish It

**1** Fold the ribbon in half, and mark the center point. Using fabric glue, squeeze a small amount onto the center mark on the ribbon. Place it at the center of the needlebook at the stitching line that is holding the pages to the cover, as shown. Let dry.

**2** Trim the ends of the ribbon on the diagonal so they will not fray.

**3** Fill the inside pages of the needle-book with your embroidery needles.

# HIDING A KNOT OR AN END

When sewing, you often will want to hide your ends between the 2 layers of fabric so that your project will look neat.

**At the start of a project:**

Tie a double knot at the end of your thread. Open up the 2 layers of fabric, and poke your needle from between the layers through to the outside of the project. Pull it through until the knot catches. Begin stitching.

**At the end of the project:**

Take your last stitch going through 1 layer of fabric only. Pull the threaded needle to the inside, and take 2 small stitches on top of one of the threads inside. Cut the thread, poking the end toward the inside of the project.

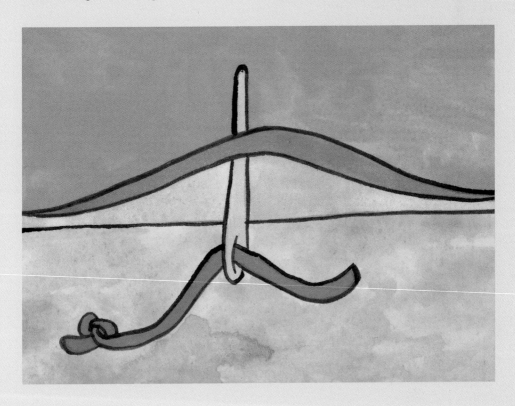

# Sew Pincushion

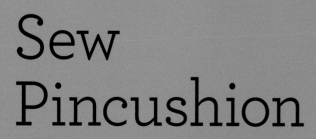

*A pincushion is a necessary tool for sewing and stitching. It is nice to make one so that you can have a handmade pincushion in your favorite color. You could stitch many different words—pins, needles, stitch, create, or your name—if you don't want to stitch sew.*

*The same steps can be used to make larger projects, such as a pillow for your bed.*

# Set Up

**1** Draw a 6˝ × 6˝ square on each color of felt. Cut along the drawn lines using your fabric scissors.

**2** Using an erasable marker, write the word *Sew* in the center of the felt piece that will be the top of the pincushion.

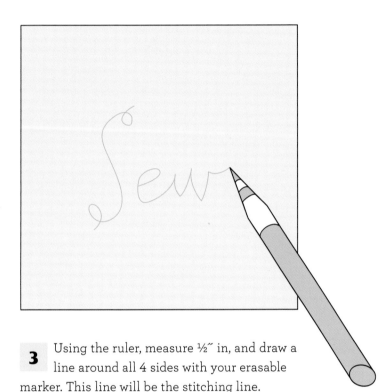

**3** Using the ruler, measure ½˝ in, and draw a line around all 4 sides with your erasable marker. This line will be the stitching line.

# Stitch It

**1** Using all 6 strands of cotton embroidery floss or a single strand of Persian wool, stitch the word *Sew* in **stem stitch**. Make your stitches about ⅛˝ long.

**2** Sew stars in **straight stitch** around the word *Sew*, keeping them within the drawn lines. The stars can have 5 or more legs (stitches) and can be from ¼˝ to ½˝.

**Stitches used:**

stem stitch (page 43)
straight stitch (page 45)
running stitch (page 40)

## Materials
*Makes 1 pincushion.*

- Wool felt in 2 colors
- White paper
- Embroidery scissors
- Chenille needle
- 1 skein embroidery floss or Persian (crewel) wool
- Erasable fabric marker
- Ruler
- Fiberfill stuffing

# Finish It

**1** Pin the 2 felt pieces together. Be sure your nice embroidery is facing up.

**2** About 1½˝ in from a corner of the felt, use a **running stitch** to sew along the drawn line. Sandwich the knot between the 2 layers of felt to hide the knot (see Hiding a Knot, page 51). When you run out of sewing thread, end your short thread with a stitched knot between the layers of felt (see Starting and Stopping, page 34).

**3** Continue around the square. When you are about 2˝ away from the beginning of the stitching, park your needle on 1 layer of the felt.

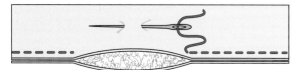

**Parked needle**

**4** Follow the manufacturer's instructions to remove the erasable marks completely. If you use water to remove the marks, let the felt dry before stuffing the pincushion. Wet felt can easily stretch out of shape.

**5** Stuff the pincushion firmly with the filling.

**6** Pick up the threaded needle again, and sew the opening closed using running stitches.

# Backpack Tags

At school, it can be so confusing to find your backpack—especially if yours is the same color as another friend's pack. Stitch your very own backpack tag so yours will be easy to spot. Backpack tags can also be used for luggage, and they make nice gifts.

ALEX

# Make It

**1** Use your ruler to draw a rectangle 2½″ × 3″ on 2 pieces of felt. Cut out the rectangles using fabric scissors.

**2** Using the erasable marking pen, write your initials or your name in the center of 1 of the rectangles, leaving about 1″ empty around the letters.

**Note:** You could also write your initials on 1 rectangle and your name on the other.

## Supplies:

*Makes 1 tag.*

- Wool felt in 2 colors
- Embroidery floss in 2 colors
- Erasable marking pen
- Ruler
- Paper and pencil
- Pins
- Fabric scissors
- Embroidery scissors
- Size 20 chenille needle
- Spray bottle with water
- ¼ yard of ⅜″-wide grosgrain ribbon

# Stitch It

**1** Cut 20″ of embroidery floss from the skein. Thread a needle with the floss, and tie a double knot in the end.

**2** Sew the letters in **back-stitch**. Try to make each stitch about ⅛″ long.

**3** Pin the 2 rectangles together with wrong sides together. Your knots will be on the inside, between the layers.

NAME

**4** Sew the pieces together around the outside with a **running stitch**. Your stitches should be approximately ¼″ long. Press with an iron. **(Get an adult to help.)**

**5** Follow the manufacturer's directions to remove the erasable marks.

# Finish It

**You may want to ask an adult for help with this step.**

**1** At 1 end of the backpack tag, mark the center point using the erasable marker. The point should be approximately ½″ in from the edge.

**2** Using the sharp point of your embroidery scissors, poke through both layers of felt to make a small hole. Using your embroidery scissors, cut a small slit through both layers of felt. The slit should be a little wider than your ribbon.

Cut here. ½″

**3** Trim each end of the ribbon at an angle. Insert the ribbon in the slit.

**4** To attach the tag, pull the ribbon through the zipper pull on your backpack, and then tie the ribbon tails together.

# Love Heart Pillow

*Stitching a LOVE heart pillow is such nice way to say "I Love You" to a special person in your life. You could take the same idea, make the heart smaller, and fill it with potpourri to make a sachet. A sachet is a small bag filled with a mixture of dried flowers and spices (potpourri), or something nice smelling, that is placed among clothes or bed and bath linens to give them a pleasant scent. Moms and aunts like them.*

**Supplies:**
*Makes 1 pillow.*

- 2 pieces of rose-colored felt, 18˝ × 18˝ each
- 1 skein of dark red embroidery floss
- Size 20 chenille needle
- Fabric scissors
- Embroidery scissors
- Craft scissors
- Sewing pins
- Erasable fabric marker
- Fiberfill

# Set Up

**1** Photocopy the heart template (page 121), enlarging it 200%. Cut out the paper heart template using craft scissors.

**2** Lay the 2 pieces of felt on top of each other, lining up the edges. Pin the heart template to both layers. With fabric scissors, neatly cut around the heart through both layers.

**3** With the erasable marker, write or print the word *LOVE* in the center of 1 of the felt hearts. Practice first by writing the word on the paper template.

# Stitch It

**1** Using a **backstitch**, sew the word *LOVE* over your handwriting. Stitch each letter separately, securing the thread on the back of the felt before moving on to the next letter (see Starting and Stopping, page 34).

**2** Pin the 2 felt hearts together. Be sure your *LOVE* stitching is on the outside.

**3** Thread your needle with a new length of floss. Hide the knot in your floss between the layers (see Hide the Knot, page 51). Stitch the hearts together using a **whipstitch**. Leave a 5˝ opening on 1 side near the bottom point.

# Finish It

**1** Stuff the heart with fiberfill. Use a capped pen or a knitting needle to push the stuffing into the V of the heart.

**2** Whipstitch the opening closed.

# BLOCKING TO FINISH

The last part of stitching most designs is finishing; this step is called blocking. When you block, you wet the fabric and pull it straight again. This removes any marks or wrinkles and settles the stitches into their final position so they look even. Fill a small, clean spray bottle with water. Place a thick bath towel on a flat surface like a table, stuffed chair, or mattress in an area where you can let your embroidery dry undisturbed. Lay the embroidery on the towel faceup, and spray it with water so that it is damp all over. With your hands, gently pull the fabric straight, smooth, and flat. If necessary, place straight pins along the edges of the fabric to hold it in place until it is dry.

# Owl Stuffie

*Who doesn't love a stuffie to cuddle with? Making it yourself makes it so much more special. For this project I used purchased wool felt, but feel free to use your own homemade felt (see Felting, page 17).*

# Set It Up

**1** Photocopy the owl pattern (page 120), enlarging it 150%. The enlarged pattern will fit on an 8½″ × 11″ piece of paper. If you like, you can draw your own animal. Just be sure the design will fit on the felt.

**2** Using craft scissors, cut around the paper patterns. Lay 1 of your pieces of felt on a flat surface, and pin the pattern piece to it. Cut around it with fabric scissors.

**Cut 2 bodies**—1 from each color.

**Cut 2 wings** from 1 color.

**Cut 2 toes** from 1 color.

**Cut 2 ears** from 1 color.

---

### TIP

*To conserve fabric, place your pattern pieces close to the edge of your felt. Then you can save the larger remnants (that is the sewing term for small pieces) for other projects.*

---

**3** Using the dressmaker's tracing paper method (page 47), transfer the eyes, nose, and mouth from the paper pattern to 1 body piece for the front of the owl. You can also draw them yourself with the erasable fabric marker, giving your owl its own personality.

**Stitches used:**

satin stitch (page 44)
backstitch (page 42)
seed stitch (page 41)
running stitch (page 40)

## Materials
*Makes 1 owl.*

- Wool felt in 3 colors (I used salmon, yellow, and light brown.)
- Embroidery floss in 2 colors (I used dark orange and dark brown.)
- Chenille or embroidery needle
- Craft scissors
- Fabric scissors
- Embroidery scissors
- Owl pattern (page 120)
- Pins
- Erasable fabric marker
- Dressmaker's transfer paper
- Fiberfill stuffing
- Spray bottle filled with water
- Pencil

# Stitch It

**Note:** *Use all 6 strands of embroidery floss for this project.*

## Embroider the Face

**1** Eyes: Thread the needle with a 20˝ length of dark brown embroidery floss, and make a double knot (page 34) at the end of the thread. Fill in each eye using a *satin stitch*. End the thread on the back of the felt (see Starting and Stopping, page 34).

**2** Nose and mouth: Thread the needle with 20˝ of dark brown embroidery floss, and make a double knot at the end of the thread. Following the lines, embroider the mouth and nose using a *backstitch*. End the stitch on the back, as before.

## Embroider and Attach the Wings

**1** To make sure you sew the decorative stitches to the correct side of each wing, first lay the wing pieces onto the body, lining up the edges. Mark the right side of each piece with the erasable marker.

**2** Thread the needle with 20˝ of dark orange embroidery floss, and tie a double knot at the end of the thread. Fill in each wing piece with *seed stitches*. Keep the starting and ending knots on the wrong side of each piece. Your stitches should be about ⅜˝ in from the edges.

**3** Attach the wings. Pin the wings on the body piece with the embroidered face. Using a *running stitch*, sew the inside edge of the wings to the body.

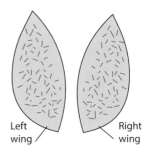

Left wing

Right wing

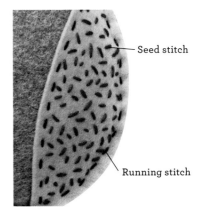

Seed stitch

Running stitch

# Put It Together

**1** Pin the owl body pieces together with the right sides facing out.

**2** Slip the ears in between the body pieces and pin. The bottom of the ear should be slipped ½˝ in between the 2 layers at the top of the head.

**3** Pin the feet between the wings at the bottom of the owl on the right side of the front piece. Match up the bottom edges of the feet with the bottom of the body.

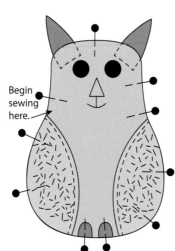

Begin sewing here.

**4** Thread the needle with dark brown embroidery floss, making a double knot at 1 end. Begin sewing the pieces together using a ***running stitch***. Begin at the top of a wing, on 1 side of the owl. Make your stitches about ¼˝ long.

**Note:** Remember to hide the starting and ending knots (page 51).

**5** Sew around the entire body, leaving a 3˝ opening for stuffing. Be sure to catch the ears in your stitching at the top of the head and toes at the bottom of the body. Park your needle (page 54) in the top layer of the owl to hold it.

# Finish It

**1** Carefully stuff the owl as full as you want it, using the eraser end of the pencil to help poke the stuffing firmly.

**2** Pick up your needle, and close the opening using a ***running stitch***.

**3** Finish by taking the thread to the back of the top layer only. Make a stitched knot (page 34) on 1 of the running stitch threads, so it will not show on the outside. Trim the floss close to the felt so it won't stick out the side.

**4** Remove the erasable marker marks, following the manufacturer's directions.

# EMBROIDERING YOUR OWN ARTWORK

Make your own artwork even more special by embroidering over it. To transfer one of your own drawings or paintings to fabric, scan the painting into your computer, and print it out on fabric transfer paper, like Lesley Riley's TAP Transfer Artist Paper from C&T Publishing (see Sources for Supplies, page 127). If you don't have a computer, ask a copy shop to photocopy your design onto transfer paper. Handle the printed transfer paper carefully so the color doesn't crack or flake off. Follow the directions on the transfer paper package to iron the design onto smooth, tightly woven cotton muslin. When the design is completely transferred, peel off the paper backing, and allow the fabric to cool. Decorate your artwork with your favorite stitches, then frame. **Because you use an iron, have an adult help you.**

# Looped Stitches

When first experimenting with free-form stitching (see Basic Free-Form Embroidery, page 38), it is easy to catch a thread with your needle when you weren't supposed to, which can create an unwanted loop or a knot. For the stitches in this chapter, you create a loop of thread on purpose.

Looped stitches are more decorative than straight stitches. You can combine them with straight stitches to make intricate embroideries or use them on their own to make simpler projects.

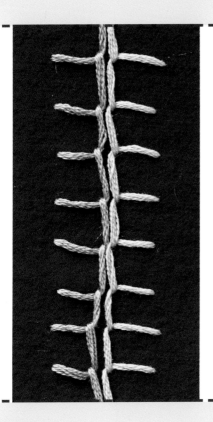

# Blanket Stitch

The blanket stitch looks like a bunch of J's hooked together. You can change the lengths of the J's of blanket stitch to make up your own patterns—1 short, 1 long, or whatever you can dream up. A blanket stitch can be sewn on the main area of your fabric, like other stitches, or along the edge of the fabric to decorate it or bind it so it will not fray.

## Did You Know?

If you sew blanket stitches very close together, it becomes buttonhole stitch. This is the stitch used to make buttonholes before sewing machines were invented.

## Sewing a Blanket Stitch on Fabric

**1** Secure your thread on the back of the fabric using a double knot (page 34), and bring the needle to the front (A). Pull the thread all the way through.

**2** Working from left to right, insert your needle down into the fabric (B), and make a scooping stitch to bring it to the front (C). Make sure the thread is looped under the needle when you pull the needle through. A j-shaped loop will form.

**3** Repeat Step 2 (the scoop stitch) to the right of your first stitch, pushing the needle in at B and back to the front at C, to make the next stitch. Space the stitches evenly (see Tip, page 46). Continue until you have sewn as many blanket stitches as you want.

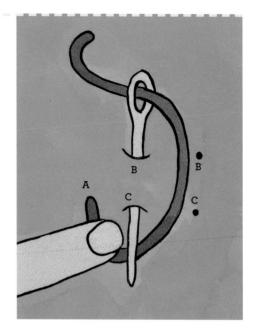

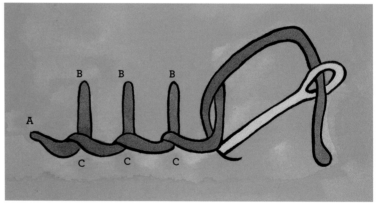

**The Amazing Stitching Handbook for Kids**

## Sewing a Blanket Stitch along an Edge

**1** Secure your thread on the back of the fabric with a double knot (page 34) very close to the edge (A). Bring the needle to the front, and pull the thread all the way through.

**2** Insert your needle down into the fabric (B), and make a scooping stitch to bring it out just beyond the edge. Make sure the thread is looped under the needle when you pull the needle through, and a j-shaped loop will form.

**3** Carefully pull the thread all the way through until the j-shaped loop just touches the edge of the fabric. Space the stitches evenly (see Spacing Stitches Evenly, page 46). If you pull too hard and the edge puckers, slip your needle under the thread and loosen it so the thread and fabric lie flat.

**4** Continue working from left to right until your edge is complete.

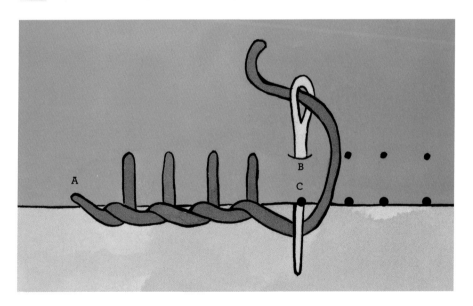

## Finish

Insert your needle down into the fabric at the corner of the last j (see the illustration, page 68), and weave it under the stitches on the back (see Stopping and Starting, page 34).

# Chain Stitch

Chain stitch is a lot of fun. It goes quickly and can be used for either outlining or filling in shapes. It looks nice in circular and natural-shaped motifs, such as flowers, leaves, and animals.

**1** Secure your thread on the back of the fabric with a double knot (page 34), and bring it to the front (A). Pull the thread through.

**2** Insert your needle down into the fabric (B), as close to A as you can without going into the same hole, and make a scooping stitch to bring it to the front (C). Make sure the thread is looped under the needle when you pull the needle through.

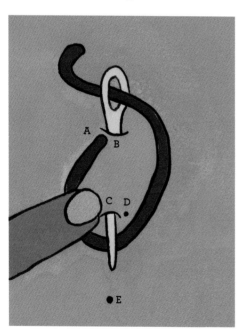

**3** Carefully pull the thread all the way through to form a loop like a link in a chain.

**4** To make the next chain stitch, insert the needle into the fabric (D) as close to C (inside the loop you just made) as you can without going into the same hole. Take another scoop stitch from D to E, catching the thread loop under the needle as before.

**5** Continue stitching until you have sewn all the chain stitches you want.

**6** To finish, insert your needle down into the fabric just below the last chain, taking a small stitch to anchor the bottom of the last loop, as shown.

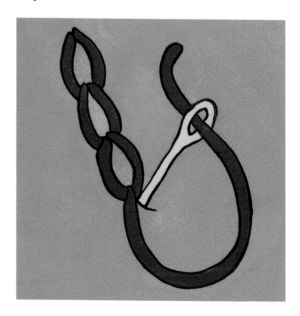

**7** Finish by weaving the thread under the stitches on the back (see Weaving the Ends, page 34).

# Lazy Daisy Stitch

The lazy daisy is actually a group of separate chain stitches arranged in a circle to look like a flower. The individual chain stitches form the petals. **IT IS SOMETIMES CALLED DETACHED CHAIN STITCH.**

You can also sew chain stitches separately on either side of a line of stem stitches, and they will look like leaves along a stem.

Here's a lazy daisy stitch completed, and the points A, B, C, and D marked for making the second chain stitch.

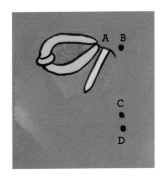

**1** To make a stitch, secure your thread on the back of the fabric using a double knot (page 34), and come up where you would like to begin the first stitch (A). Pull the thread through.

**2** Insert your needle down into the fabric (B), and make a scooping stitch to bring it to the front (C). Make sure the thread is looped under the needle when you pull the needle through.

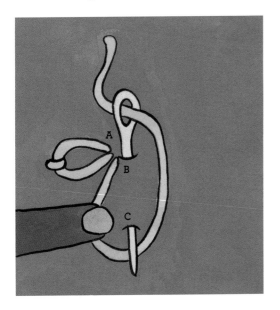

**3** Carefully pull the thread all the way through to form a loop like a link in a chain. To anchor the end of the loop, take a small stitch by inserting the needle (D).

**4** Sew individual chain stitches around in a circle, anchoring each loop with a small stitch and always beginning each chain stitch close to the center of the flower. The petals of the flower will radiate around the center with the points A and B of each petal close together.

# Featherstitch

Featherstitch is similar to chain stitch, but it has a more open look to it. **MAKING A FEATHER-STITCH IS LIKE DOING A SQUARE DANCE** where the threads swing from one side of an imaginary line to the other. When sewn with lots of space between the stitches, the featherstitch has a decorative appearance like a fern plant or coral in the ocean. It can be stitched in straight lines to make stripes, or as a decorative border for the hem of a skirt or pants, or along the edge of a pillow.

**1** Sew the stitches along a drawn (or imaginary) line. Secure your thread on the back of the fabric using a double knot (page 34), and bring it to the front (A). Pull the thread through.

**2** Insert your needle down into the fabric (B), off to the side of your stitching line. Make a scooping stitch to bring it to the front on the stitching line (C). Make sure the thread is looped under the needle when you pull the needle through.

**3** Carefully pull the thread all the way through to form a loop that looks like a hook, as shown.

**4** To make the second featherstitch, insert the needle into the fabric on the other side of your stitching line (D), and make a scooping stitch to bring it to the front on the stitching line (E).

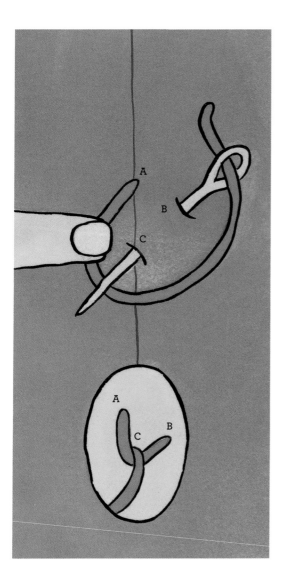

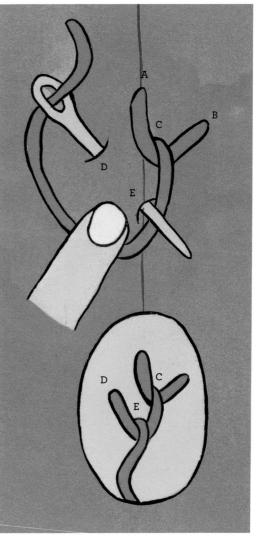

Two completed featherstitches

**5** To make the third featherstitch, insert the needle into the fabric (F) on the same side of the stitching line as the first stitch. Make a scooping stitch to bring the thread to the front on the stitching line (G).

**6** Continue stitching until you have created all the featherstitches you want. Remember to come up to the front of the fabric along the stitching line, and to alternate stitches on each side of the line.

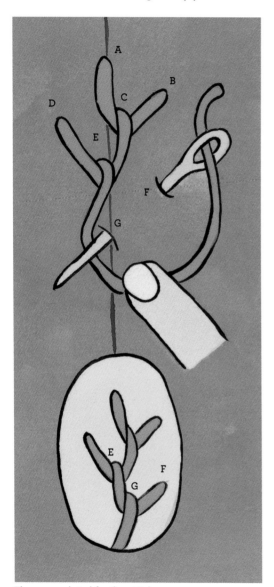

Three completed featherstitches

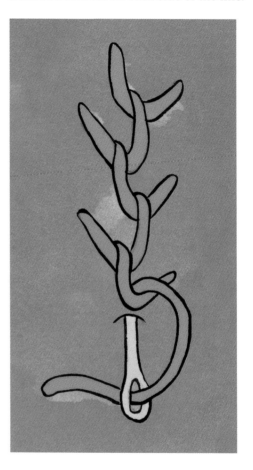

**7** To finish, insert your needle down into the fabric at the bottom of the last hook, and take a small stitch to anchor it. Secure the thread under the stitches on the back (see Ending Stitches, page 34).

The Amazing Stitching Handbook for Kids

# Bookmarks

*Embroidered bookmarks are a fun project to make and give. They are very quick to stitch. Make several in different colors using all the stitches you know, and save them for gifts. If you like to give books as gifts, a handmade bookmark is the perfect addition.*

**Stitches used:**

blanket stitch
(page 67)

chain stitch
(page 70)

lazy daisy stitch
(page 71)

featherstitch
(page 72)

(or any of the
stitches that you
have learned)

## Materials

*Makes 1 bookmark.*

- Wool felt
- Embroidery floss
- Chenille or embroidery needle
- Fabric scissors
- Embroidery scissors
- Ruler
- Erasable marker
- Steam iron

# Set Up

**1** Using a ruler and an erasable marker, measure and draw a rectangle 2˝ × 6˝ on a piece of wool felt. Cut along the lines.

**2** Draw a straight line down the center of the bookmark lengthwise, using the ruler and erasable marker.

# Stitch It

**1** Stitch the bookmarks using the different stitches you have learned. Begin and end ¼˝ from the edges of the bookmark. You can use any of these stitches to sew along the drawn line.

> *Running stitch • Outline stitch • Backstitch • Chain stitch • Blanket stitch • Featherstitch*

**2** Here are some additional stitches that will look great on your bookmark.

> *Lazy daisy stitch for flowers • Lazy daisy stitch for leaves • Satin stitch • Straight stitch*

# Finish It

Fill the iron with water and set it to steam. Let the iron heat up. When it begins steaming, hold it about 1˝ above the bookmark so that the steam helps to even out and set the stitches. **Have an adult help you with the iron.**

# Dots Hoop Art

If you are a crafty kid, you probably know how to paint. Why not combine your new love of embroidery with painting? Fabric paints are available at craft stores in hundreds of colors. Paint any design on a piece of cotton or linen following the manufacturer's instructions. Decorate the design with embroidery. This simple design is made of polka dots. A plastic embroidery hoop serves as an inexpensive circular frame.

**Stitch used:**

chain stitch (page 70)

## Materials:

- 6″ embroidery hoop
- ¼ yard white fabric, such as bleached muslin
- Erasable marker
- Fabric paints—I used periwinkle, azalea, lime, sunshine yellow, and mandarin orange colors.
- Newspaper or drop cloth to paint on
- Small paintbrush
- Lid from a deli container or plastic plate
- 3 colors of embroidery floss—I used orange, green, and purple.
- Fabric scissors
- Embroidery scissors
- Pencil
- Coins
- Craft glue
- Clear plastic bag

# Set Up

**1** Iron the fabric, **with an adult's help**. Place the bottom half of the hoop (the smaller part) on the fabric. Using a pencil, trace around the outside of the hoop.

**2** Arrange the coins on the fabric in a pleasing pattern inside the pencil circle.

**3** Using the erasable marker, draw around the coins.

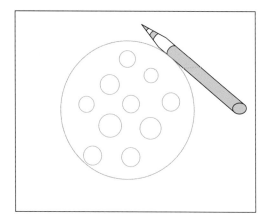

**4** Cover the table with newspaper or a drop cloth.

**5** Squeeze a *small* amount of each paint color onto a plastic lid or thick paper plate. Paint the circles with different colors of craft paint. Let dry.

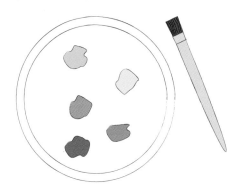

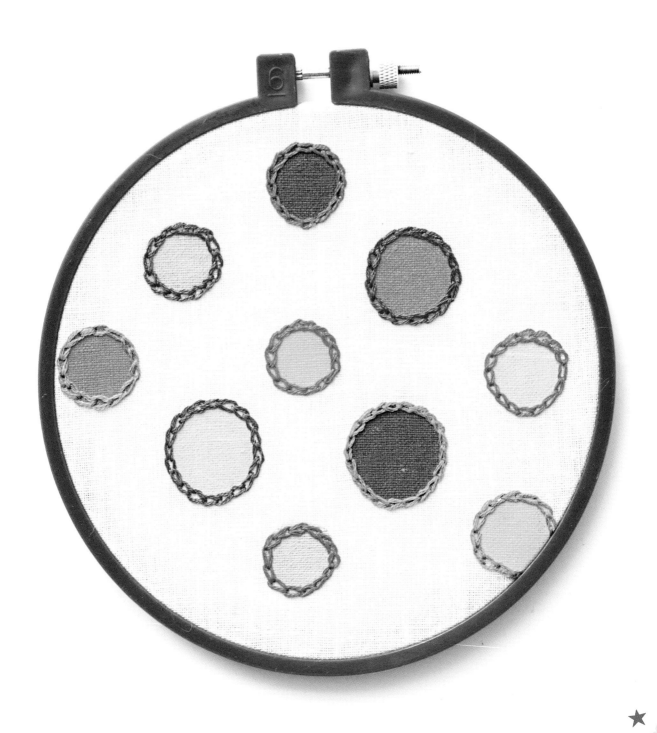

# Stitch It

**1** Using various colors of embroidery floss, sew a *chain stitch* around each dot. I used 3 strands of floss (see Separating the Strands, page 11). Your stitches should be approximately ⅛″ long.

**2** Begin and end each stitched circle before moving on to the next painted dot (see Starting and Stopping, page 34). Do not draw the floss across the back of the fabric, or the thread may show on the front.

# Finish It

**1** Lay the painted and stitched fabric on top of the smaller piece of the hoop. Lay the top of the hoop on top of the fabric, and sandwich your stitched fabric between it. Make sure that the dots are centered in the hoop. Place the screw that tightens the top part of the hoop at the top of your "framed" embroidery.

**2** Pull the fabric tightly so that the embroidery doesn't sag. When you are happy with the placement, tighten the screw.

**3** Lay your hoop upside down on a table. Using craft glue, apply a small line of glue on the back of the smaller hoop. Pull the fabric over the glue.

**4** Lay a plastic bag over the fabric and hoop. Place a stack of books on top. Let the glue dry.

**5** When it is completely dry, remove the plastic bag. Trim the excess fabric close to the hoop.

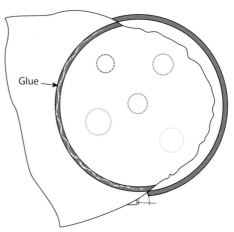

Glue →

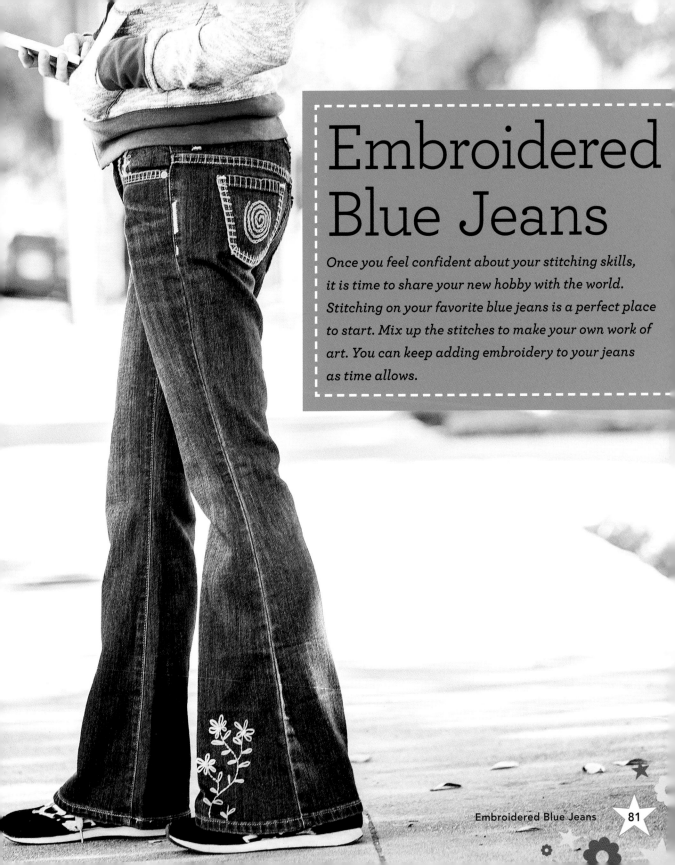

# Embroidered Blue Jeans

*Once you feel confident about your stitching skills, it is time to share your new hobby with the world. Stitching on your favorite blue jeans is a perfect place to start. Mix up the stitches to make your own work of art. You can keep adding embroidery to your jeans as time allows.*

**Stitches used:**

blanket stitch (page 67)

chain stitch (page 70)

lazy daisy stitch (page 71)

## Materials

- Blue jeans
- Chenille or embroidery needle
- Cotton embroidery floss in assorted colors
- Thimble
- Embroidery scissors
- Erasable marker or fine-line permanent marker

# Set Up

**1** Take a look at your jeans, examining all the seams and pockets. A good place to start is to stitch over the seams to create an easy decoration.

**2** Using the erasable marker or permanent marker, draw some motifs on your jeans to use as stitching lines. You can make up your own or use the ideas provided (see Motifs, pages 122–126). If you're using a permanent marker, you'll need to stitch over the marking lines so they won't show.

# Stitch It

**1** Using all 6 strands of floss, sew a *blanket stitch* around the openings at the pockets—both front and back. Hide the knots in the inside of the pockets or back of the fabric.

**2** Decorate the seams with your favorite stitches. There is no need for an embroidery hoop because the fabric is very stiff.

**3** Using the different stitches you have learned, stitch over the motifs you drew on your jeans.

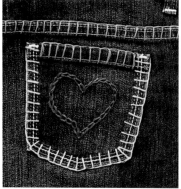

**4** It is fun to stitch spontaneously without any guidelines. Let your needle be your pencil, and stitch vines, flowers, and leaves.

# Finish It

**1** If you used an erasable marker, follow the manufacturer's directions to remove the marks.

**2** Wear your jeans with a smile, and tell your friends you decorated them yourself.

# Phone or MP3 Player Cozy

*Do you love carrying your music and listening to it whenever you have a free minute? This little cozy will protect your device when you are carrying it. The wool felt is nice and squishy and will cushion it. I made my daughter, Julia, an embroidered carrying case for her iPod. She keeps it safe in her backpack while she is at school.*

**Stitches used:**

featherstitch (page 72)

lazy daisy stitch (page 71)

satin stitch (page 44)

blanket stitch (page 67)

**Materials:**

- • • ○ 3 pieces of wool felt or homemade felt from a sweater
- • • ○ Embroidery floss in 3 colors
- • • ○ Button, ¾˝ diameter
- • • ○ Pins
- • • ○ Craft scissors
- • • ○ Fabric scissors
- • • ○ Embroidery scissors
- • • ○ Paper
- • • ○ Pencil
- • • ○ Ruler
- • • ○ Erasable marker
- • • ○ Chenille needle

# Set It Up

*Use craft scissors to cut paper and fabric scissors to cut felt.*

**1** Make the pattern pieces. Lay the device you're making the cozy for on the paper, and trace around all 4 edges with the pencil. Using a ruler, draw a line around all 4 sides 1˝ away from the traced outline, making square corners. Cut out the pattern along the outer lines.

**2** Pin the pattern to your felt and cut around it. Repeat this step to cut a second piece the same size.

**3** Using the ruler, measure down 1¼˝ from a narrow end, and draw a line with the erasable marker. Trim the piece along the line. This will be the front of the cozy.

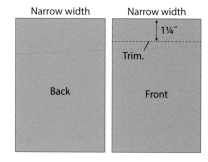

**4** To make a top flap to fit your cozy, first measure across your front or back felt piece to find the width. Draw a rectangle on paper that is as wide as your measured width and 2¾˝ high. Cut along the lines on the paper. Pin this flap pattern to the felt and cut the piece.

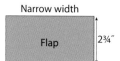

# Stitch It

**NOTE:** *Use all 6 strands of floss for this project. Tie a knot at the beginning and end of the floss (see Starting and Stopping, page 34).*

**1** Using the erasable marker, draw 2 lines resembling flower stems on the front piece of felt. My stems were about 2˝ and 2½˝ long and slightly curved.

**2** Thread the needle with floss for the stems. Bring the thread to the front at the top of 1 of the lines you drew for your stem. Stitch the stems in a **featherstitch**. The bottom of the stems should end about ½˝ from the edge of the felt.

**3** Using the flower color, stitch the flower petals in **lazy daisy stitch**, leaving an opening at the center of the stitches.

**4** Stitch the center of each flower in **satin stitch**.

**5** Finish the front piece with **blanket stitch** on the upper edge. Begin at the upper left edge, and hide the knot at the back of the work about ⅛˝ in from the edge. Sew a blanket stitch, making your stitches about ⅜˝ apart and ⅜˝ long (see Working Blanket Stitch along an Edge, page 69).

# Finish It

## Join the Front and Back

**1** Pin the front embroidered piece to the back piece, lining up the side and bottom edges neatly. Beginning at the upper right corner, anchor your knot on the inside of the case. Join the pieces using a blanket stitch around the 3 edges, ending at upper left. Sew 3 stitches at each corner—1 at each corner side perpendicular to each edge and 1 stitched diagonally at the corner.

**2** Hide the ending knot on the inside of the case.

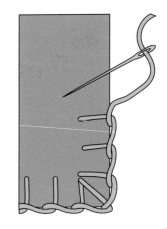

## Embroider the Flap

Embroider the flap with blanket stitches along the 2 short sides and 1 long edge.

## Flap Buttonhole

**1** On the wrong side of the flap, make a mark ⅞˝ above the center of the long stitched edge. You can fold the flap in half to find the center, and then measure ⅞˝ from the lower stitched edge and make a mark.

**2** Draw a 1˝ line on the inside of the flap, centered over the mark and parallel to the long edge.

Midpoint

⅞˝

**3** Using the embroidery scissors, cut the buttonhole opening along this line.

**4** Sew a blanket stitch around the buttonhole slit, making small stitches about ⅛˝ and spaced ⅛˝ apart.

**5** At each end of the slit, place 4 stitches forming a semicircle around the slit.

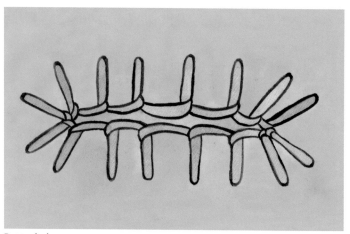

**Buttonhole**

## Attach the Flap

**1** Pin the flap to the cozy at the upper edge.

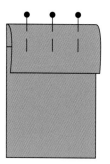

**2** Sew the 2 layers together using a blanket stitch. Begin stitching ½˝ below the left corner, placing 3 stitches to turn the corner as done at the bottom of the case (Step 1, Join the Front and Back, page 87). Sew across the top and finish ½˝ below the right corner.

**3** Poke a pin through the center of the buttonhole opening onto the layers below. Mark this point on the front cozy piece with the erasable marker.

**4** Sew the button on this mark (see How to Sew on a Button, page 89).

# HOW TO SEW ON A BUTTON

**1 CHOOSE** a needle that is thin enough to go through the holes of the button.

**2 CUT** a piece of floss about 15˝ long. Separate 3 strands of embroidery floss. Thread the needle with the floss, and put a knot in the end.

**3 TAKE** 2 small stitches on the back of the fabric where you want to place the button. Bring the needle to the front.

**4 POKE** the needle up through 1 of the holes, from the back of the button to the front. Then push the needle back down into the hole next to it and through the fabric.

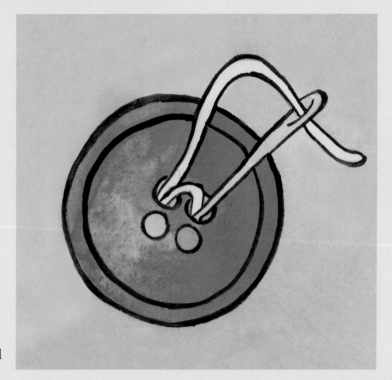

**5 POKE** the tip of the needle up through the fabric and the third hole of the button. Go back down through the last hole. (If your button has only 2 holes, just go in and out of the same holes.)

**6 REPEAT** this until you've stitched through all the holes 5 or 6 times. Bring the needle to the back of the fabric, and take a few small stitches on the inside to anchor the thread. Trim it close to the fabric.

# Embellished Fabric Picture

*So many beautiful fabrics are available in fabric stores. Use a rectangle of fabric as your canvas. Outline the different motifs with your favorite stitches. It is easiest to stitch on home decor fabrics because they are loosely woven and your thread and needle will glide through them. Avoid quilting fabric, as it is tightly woven and difficult to stitch through.*

The Amazing Stitching Handbook for Kids

# Set Up

**1** Remove the cardboard backing from your picture frame. Hold on to the cardboard; you will use it later.

**2** Lay the frame on the fabric. Move it around until you decide which part you want to include in your picture. Using an erasable marker, draw around the inside of the frame.

**3** Cut the fabric, leaving a margin of 2˝ beyond the drawn lines on all side. This will give you space to place your hoop.

## Stitches used:

stem stitch (page 43)
blanket stitch (page 67)
chain stitch (page 70)
featherstitch (page 72)
seed stitch (page 41)
straight stitch (page 45)

## Materials

- ½ yard of home decor fabric*

- Embroidery floss in several colors**

- Chenille or embroidery needle

- Picture frame

- Erasable marker

- Fabric scissors

- Embroidery scissors

- Iron

*For your home decor fabric, look for simple fabric designs with bold shapes that can easily be embroidered. Geometric prints with triangles, squares, and circles will make a more graphic picture. Floral prints will look soft and feminine.

**Choose embroidery floss colors that will look pretty and stand out from the design on your fabric. Collect an assortment of colors—they are your crayons and markers.

# Stitch It

**1** Decide which stitches you want to use. To outline shapes, **stem**, **blanket**, and **chain stitch** work nicely. To fill shapes, use **feather**, **seed**, and **straight stitch**.

**2** Begin stitching. You can use all 6 strands of floss for a heavy design. For a lighter look, separate the strands and stitch with 1, 2, or 3 strands of floss (see Separating the Stands, page 11). Use an embroidery hoop if your stitches are getting bunchy and gathered.

# Finish It

**1** Trim the stitched fabric ½˝ outside the marked frame lines. Block your design (see Blocking, page 59) with the fabric facedown to neaten the stitching.

**2** Place the fabric, right side up, on the cardboard backing that came with the picture frame. Slip the fabric and cardboard into the frame behind the glass. Tighten the hardware to enclose your stitched fabric.

**3** Hang your embroidered picture in your room.

# EMBROIDERY AROUND THE WORLD

Almost every culture in the world uses embroidery to decorate clothing and household items. Here are just a few examples. In JAPAN, kimonos and obis (sashes) are often decorated with a combination of embroidery and fabric painting. The CHINESE discovered the secret of making silk thread and fabric from silkworm cocoons and have used silk for embroidery for thousands of years. Satin stitches and knotted stitches are frequently used in traditional Chinese embroidery.

INDIA AND PAKISTAN have an amazing number of techniques and traditions for embroidery. Shisha embroidery is the most famous: small round mirror pieces are enclosed within embroidery stitches to make colorful, sparkly fabrics. Because AFGHANISTAN is one of the countries along the historic Silk Road, its embroidery includes materials and designs from many countries: silk from China, cotton from Pakistan and India, carpet motifs from other Middle Eastern countries. Nomadic tribes still decorate their clothing and animal gear with embroidery today.

Traditional embroidery throughout EASTERN EUROPE features cross-stitch sewn in red and black threads on white fabric, although different color schemes are used to indicate different regions. Elaborate satin-stitch floral embroidery is one of the first things people notice when they see traditional folk costumes from SCANDINAVIA. These costumes were reinvented in the late nineteenth century by people wanting to explore and celebrate their national heritages. In NORWAY, embroidery shares many of the same floral motifs with a popular folk-painting technique called rosemaling.

A traditional NATIVE AMERICAN type of embroidery called quillwork uses dyed, flattened porcupine quills stitched onto a tanned animal skin. Instead of thread, they use sinew (the tendons from the leg of deer, elk, or buffalo), which has to be chewed in order to stay soft enough for stitching.

Many people in MEXICO AND GUATEMALA still wear bright embroidered clothing every day. The Guatemalan woman's blouse known as a huipil features motifs that may have symbolic meanings, such as flowers to represent the beauty and bounty of the earth.

The women are wearing stitching typical of China, Japan, Mexico, Eastern Europe, and Scandinavia (left to right). The wall in the background has Indian, Asian, and Native American motifs.

# Fancy Stitches

So far, most of the stitches you have learned have been easy to do and only take one or two steps to complete. A needle and thread can be made to do many more neat tricks.

All the fancy stitches in this chapter are made by wrapping the thread around a needle (French knots and bullion knots) or wrapping the thread around another stitch (spider web and woven bars). These stitches are raised above the surface of the fabric to add texture. Fancy stitches are often used in combination with more basic stitches. There are hundreds of fancy stitches you can learn. To explore them, go to your local library or craft or needlework store, and look at the stitch dictionaries they have on their shelves. Explore embroidery sites on the Internet too.

# French Knots

French knots lend themselves to all kinds of decoration—the most common use is in the middle of lazy daisy stitches to mark the center of the flower. French knots also make perfect grapes and curly hair. You can even use them as polka dots all over a pillow or in lines as a border. Often French knots are stitched individually, starting and ending the thread for each knot. This is useful if you are working on a thin, see-through fabric where threads connecting one French knot to another might show through on the front.

**1** Secure your thread on the back of the fabric with a double knot (page 34), and bring the needle to the front (A). Pull the thread through.

**2** With a finger and thumb from your hand that is not holding the needle, pinch the thread about ½″ away from point A. Wrap the thread around the needle (in either direction) twice toward the tip of the needle.

**3** Pulling gently on the thread to hold the wraps snugly against the needle, rotate the point of the needle down toward the fabric, and insert needle (B) right next to A. (If you put the needle in the exact same hole at A, the knot will disappear through to the back.)

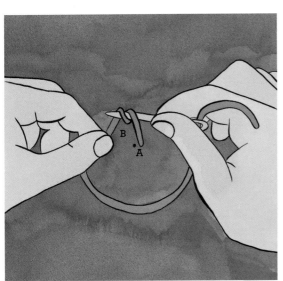

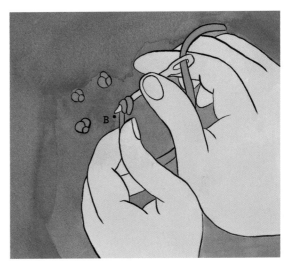

**4** Still holding the thread tight so the wraps stay against the needle, push the needle to the back of the fabric and pull through. A small knot will appear on the surface. That's a French knot!

**5** To finish, turn the fabric over so you can see the back. Right behind the French knot (so it won't show on the front), make a stitched knot (page 34).

# Bullion Knot

The bullion knot stitch is sometimes called the caterpillar stitch because it looks like … a caterpillar. It is a little tricky to learn, but once you do, you can make very long bullion knots that twist and turn every which way.

**1** Secure your thread on the back of the fabric with a double knot (page 34), and bring the needle to the front (A). Pull the thread through.

**2** Insert the needle where you want the knot to end (B), and make a scooping stitch to bring it to the front at A again. Do not pull the needle all the way through. Leave about 1˝ of the needle tip sticking out of the fabric.

**3** With a finger and thumb from your hand that is not holding the needle, pinch the thread about 2˝ away from A. Wrap the thread around the needle about 7 times, wrapping away from your body, as shown. If you wrap the wrong way, the plies of the thread will start to untwist and loosen.

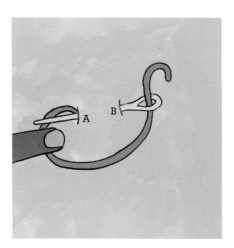

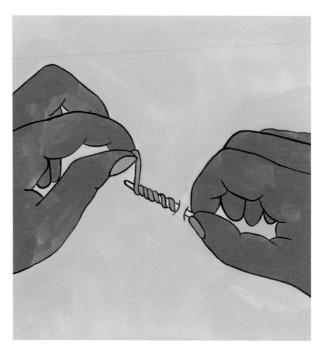

**The Amazing Stitching Handbook for Kids**

**4** Hold the wraps snugly against the needle, and gently push the needle all the way through the tunnel of the wraps, as is about to happen in the illustration. The eye of the needle will disappear into the fabric so you can't push any more.

**5** Grab the tip of the needle with the other hand. Gently pull the needle out while pushing the wraps snugly toward the fabric. Adjust the wraps with your fingers or the point of your needle so they lie flat and even.

**6** To finish, insert the needle right next to B, and pull the thread through to the back. Turn the fabric over to the back and, right behind the bullion knot (so it won't show on the front), make a stitched knot (page 34).

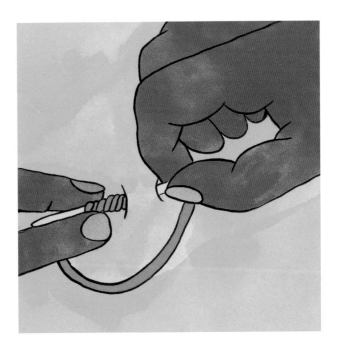

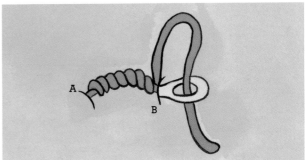

# Spider Web Stitch

The spider web stitch begins with the straight stitch. The spokes are then woven to form the web.

**1** Secure your thread on the back of the fabric with a double knot (page 34). Bring the needle to the front of the fabric (A), and pull the thread through.

**2** Make a star shape with 7 spokes ½˝ each (straight stitch, page 45). If you want your star shape to form a perfect circle, trace around a coin with an erasable marker before you stitch the spokes.

**3** Bring your needle to the front again at A.

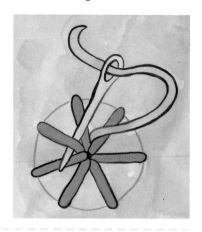

**4** Use the needle to weave over 1 spoke and under the next. Weave around in a circle, gently pulling on the thread to take up the slack. Continue weaving until the spider web is filled in as much as you like. Be careful not to pull the thread too tight so the web lies nice and flat.

**5** Use the back of the needle (the dull end) to nudge the weaving thread toward the center of the web so that the spokes are covered.

**6** To finish, insert your needle into the fabric very close to the end of 1 of the spokes, and take the thread to the back. Make a stitched knot (page 34). Trim the end, leaving a ¼˝ tail.

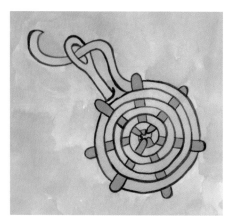

> ## TIP
> *You can work a spider web stitch using any odd number of spokes. Try experimenting with 5, 9, or 11 spokes. The larger the circle is drawn, the more spokes are needed.*

**The Amazing Stitching Handbook for Kids**

# Woven Bar

The woven bar stitch is one of several needle-weaving stitches. This stitch is similar to the spider web stitch, but instead of weaving around in a circle, you weave back and forth over two straight stitches. This makes a little piece of thin woven fabric that seems to float on the surface of the embroidery.

You can use the woven bar for leaves, petals, and clothing. Once you get the hang of this stitch, you can increase the number of straight stitches you begin with to make larger woven bars.

**1** Secure your thread on the back of the fabric with a double knot (page 34), and bring the needle to the front (A). Pull the thread all the way through, then insert the needle about 1″ away (B).

**2** Repeat to make a second stitch the same length, very close to the first stitch, but not using the same holes in the fabric.

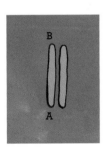

**3** Bring the needle to the front (C). Begin weaving by going over the first long stitch and under the second long stitch. When the needle goes under the second long stitch, do not go through the fabric.

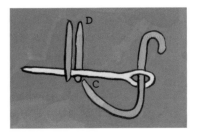

**4** Turn the needle to point in the opposite direction, and again go over the first thread and under the second thread. Continue weaving until the straight-stitch threads are completely covered.

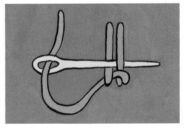

**5** Use the back of the needle (the dull end) to push the weaving threads closely together.

**6** When you are happy with the way the woven bar looks, insert the needle to the back of the fabric, very close to the end of one of the straight stitches (D). Make a stitched knot (page 34) and trim the end, leaving a ¼″ tail.

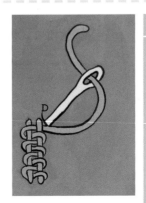

# NEEDLEWORK SAMPLERS

**NEEDLEWORK SAMPLERS HAVE BEEN MADE FOR HUNDREDS OF YEARS.** The tradition began in Europe, where the earliest known sampler is dated 1502. Historically, samplers were made by young girls and women as learning pieces for trying out new stitches. (Of course, now both boys and girls can stitch samplers if they want to.) The embroiderers passed ideas, stitches, and new patterns on to friends and family by showing and sharing their samplers among themselves.

This sharing of ideas is how different stitches traveled from one community to another. When the first colonists came to America, they brought this sampler-making tradition with them. When a girl began learning needlework, her first sampler was usually the alphabet and numbers sewn in cross-stitch. She began stitching at about the same age that she learned to read and write. **BY MAKING AN ALPHABET SAMPLER, A GIRL LEARNED TO STITCH, COUNT THREADS, AND TO CONCENTRATE.**

Most American samplers had a stitched border on the sides and across the top made with leaves and vines, flowers, or geometric patterns. Sometimes a poem, phrase, or passage from the Bible was included. Often at the bottom of the sampler, there was a scene with a house, barn, trees, farm animals, family, wildlife, and flowers. Most of the time, the sampler maker stitched her name, birthday, and year the sampler was made. Some samplers even listed all the members of the family with the dates of important family events, like births, deaths, and weddings— **A PERFECT WAY TO MAKE A VISUAL DIARY OF THE FAMILY AT A TIME WHEN THERE WERE NO PHOTOGRAPHS.**

**Early American sampler**

You can make your own sampler. To make it look traditional, find tan-colored linen to stitch on and several colors of embroidery floss. Draw a geometric or floral border around the sides and across the top of the fabric. Draw a picture of your house, your family, and animals. Add your name, birthday, and the year you make the sampler. **SEW THE PICTURES IN ANY COMBINATION OF STITCHES YOU LIKE.** You will be carrying on an age-old tradition.

# Tess's Notecard

*A few years ago, I taught some local kids to embroider. It was so much fun sharing something I love to do and listening to the girls tell stories as they stitched. One day, I received a note in the mail from Tess, one of the girls, thanking me for teaching her. I still have the card on my refrigerator. Tess's card inspired this project.*

**Stitches used:**

Spider web (page 100)

lazy daisy stitch (page 71)

French knot (page 97)

running stitch (page 40)

chain stitch (page 70)

featherstitch (page 72)

## Materials:

- ¼ yard linen or cotton fabric
- Embroidery floss in 3 colors
- Coin to trace around
- Erasable marker
- Chenille or embroidery needle
- 4˝ embroidery hoop (*optional*)
- Fabric scissors
- Embroidery scissors
- Card stock in a pretty color
- Envelope (in a size to fit your card)
- Double-stick tape

# Set Up

**1** Straighten the grain of the fabric (pages 8 and 9). Cut a 6˝ square from the fabric.

**2** To make the flower card, first use the erasable marker to trace around the coin in the center of the fabric. For the heart card, draw a heart or circle (for a flower) in the center of the fabric square using an erasable marker.

**3** Mount the fabric in the embroidery hoop, if you want to use one.

# Stitch It

*Use 6 strands of floss for stitches unless indicated otherwise. Refer to Separating the Strands (page 11) for more information.*

**1** For a flower design, use 1 of the colors of embroidery floss, stitch the center of the flower using a **spider web stitch** in the traced circle.

**2** Using a second color of embroidery floss, stitch 7 **lazy daisy** petals around the embroidered circle.

**3** Using 2 strands of a third color of embroidery floss, sew a **French knot** in between each petal.

**4** For the heart card, stitch an outer line with a **running stitch**. Stitch an inner line in **chain stitch**. Sew a **featherstitch** down the center of the heart.

# Make the Card

**1** Trim the embroidered fabric so that it is approximately 4˝ to 4½˝ square. Be sure the embroidered design is in the center of the trimmed square.

**2** Fringe the edges. With a needle or a pin, pull out the loose threads at 1 edge of the fabric and unravel it. Continue unraveling until you have about ½˝ of fringe. Continue around the 3 remaining sides.

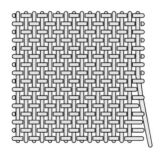

**3** Remove the erasable markings (if they are visible), following the manufacturer's directions.

**4** Block the embroidered square to neaten (page 59).

**5** Fold the cardstock in half to make a card.

**6** Using double-stick tape, attach the embroidered fabric square in the center of the card.

**7** Write a note on the card, and send it to someone special.

# THROW AN EMBROIDERY PARTY

Now that you know how much fun it is to embroider, don't you want to share it with your friends? Plan a party.

## 1. Make Invitations

For the cover of each invitation, embroider a simple design on a small piece of fabric and glue it on neatly (see Tess's Notecard, page 103). Inside, write something like this:

> *It's a party! Please come to my house to learn embroidery!*
>
> *[Date]*
>
> *[Time]*
>
> *[Your Name and Address]*
>
> *Bring 6 different colors of embroidery floss to share.*
>
> *I hope you can come!*

## 2. Pick a Project

Select something you think most of your friends would like to make that can be completed in the time you've allowed for the party. You can apply the stitches from any of the projects in this book to a small project like a felt bookmark. Make a list of the supplies you will need (aside from the embroidery floss, which your friends will be bringing). Visit your local needlework or craft store to purchase the supplies.

## 3. Make a Sample

Make up a sample project so everyone can see what he or she will be making before they get started. Have fun!

# Embellished Carry Tote

*Adding an embroidered floral felt pocket is a special way to dress up a simple canvas bag. Pack it up with all your embroidery supplies, and you'll be ready to head off to the park or a friend's house to teach them embroidery.*

# Set Up

**1** Using a ruler and erasable marker, draw a 6˝ square on the felt. Cut out the pocket square with fabric scissors.

**2** Place the coins on the felt square where you want the flowers to be. Using the erasable marker, trace around the coins.

**3** Use your ruler to draw a straight line from each circle down to the bottom of the square, ending ¼˝ away from edge.

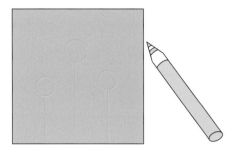

# Stitch It

**Note:** *Use all 6 strands of floss unless otherwise noted.*

**1** Using **spider web stitch**, embroider the circles using 3 different colors of floss.

**2** Using **stem stitch**, sew the stems of the flowers, ending ¼˝ from the bottom of the fabric.

**3** Using **woven bar stitch**, sew 2 leaves near the bottom of each stem. To make a leaf with a point on the end, pull the weaving thread tighter as you near the end.

**4** Add the petals around the circles. For the left flower, use 3 strands of floss and stitch the petals using *lazy daisy stitch*. For the center flower, stitch *bullion knots* with 6 strands of floss for petals. For the right flower, add *French knots* for petals, using 2 strands of floss.

**5** Using a **running stitch**, sew a straight line across the top of the pocket piece about ¼˝ from the top edge.

## Stitches used:

spider web (page 100)
stem stitch (page 43)
woven bar (page 101)
lazy daisy stitch (page 71)
bullion knots (page 98)
French knots (page 97)
running stitch (page 40)

## Materials:

- Wool felt for pocket
- Embroidery floss in 4 or more colors
- Chenille or embroidery needle
- Ruler
- Fabric scissors
- Embroidery scissors
- Three coins for tracing
- Erasable fabric marker
- Pins and pincushion
- Canvas bag, available at most craft stores

# Finish It

**1**    Block the embroidered pocket (page 59).

**2**    Iron the canvas bag to neaten.

**3**    Place the pocket in the center of 1 side of the bag, about 2¼″ down from the top edge. Pin in place on 3 sides, leaving the top free.

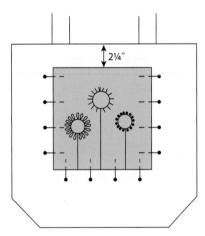

**4**    Using a running stitch, sew the patch pocket to the outside of the bag. Anchor your sewing thread inside the bag to begin. Make your stitches the same length as the running stitch you made on the top of the pocket. Sew the side and bottom edges only. Secure the thread on the inside of the bag (see Starting and Stopping, page 34).

# Patch Collection

*These patches are great for practicing different types of embroidery stitches. Use them to decorate your favorite things—bags, barrettes, hats, pants, journal, cards, backpacks, walls, windows, or Christmas trees. Templates are available for you to practice stitching (pages 122–126). Combine these small motifs to inspire more ideas for your own designs!*

## Stitches used:

All stitches—the sky is the limit!
Refer to the following pages for ideas:
Gridded Stitches (page 18)
Free-Form Stitches (page 38)
Looped Stitches (page 66)
Fancy Stitches (page 96)

## Materials

*Makes as many patches as desired.*

- Wool felt in various colors
- Small amounts of Persian wool or embroidery floss in several colors
- Chenille needle or any sharp-pointed embroidery needle with an eye that will fit your thread
- Fabric scissors
- Embroidery scissors
- Ruler or tape measure
- Erasable fabric marker or dressmaker's tracing paper in a color that will show on your felt
- Pins
- Assorted scraps of ribbon, rickrack, or seam binding (6″ to 8″ long), for hanging ornaments (*optional*)
- Fabric glue
- Iron (*optional*)

> **TIP**
>
> *Look for items you can find around the house to be used as embroidery and shape templates. Coins, jar lids, deli containers, plates, bowls, student ID cards, and many other household shapes can be traced and become design elements in your embroidery projects.*

# Set Up

**1** Choose a motif (pages 122–126) and enlarge it to the size you want on a copy machine.

**2** Transfer the motif to the felt using dressmaker's tracing paper (page 47), or draw your own design with the erasable or permanent marker. If the transfer markings aren't dark enough on the felt, use the erasable marker to draw on top of them.

**3** Trim the felt, leaving 2″ around the design so that you will be able to hold on to it while stitching.

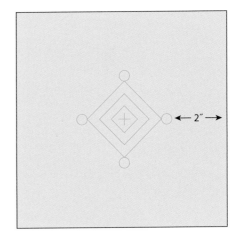

# Stitch It

**1** Choose stitches and colors. (It's not necessary to plan out your whole design before you start; in fact, it's often easier and more fun to choose the stitches and colors as you go.) To get started, refer to the Stitch Guide (page 116).

**2** Separate the strands of your embroidery floss (page 11). Experiment using different numbers of strands to create different effects. The samples shown here were made with 1 strand of Persian wool or 4 strands of embroidery floss. Sew the stitches you've chosen, referring to the stitch instructions as needed.

# Cut the Patch

**1** You can make a patch any shape you like—a circle, oval, square, rectangle, diamond, or hexagon. Use your motif as your guide for the finished shape. Trace around common household objects such as the bottom of a glass, a jar lid, a coaster, or a pack of cards.

**2** Using fabric scissors, cut the felt shape, being careful to leave a margin of at least ¼˝ to ½˝ around the embroidery lines on all sides. If you'd like to embroider a border, leave more space.

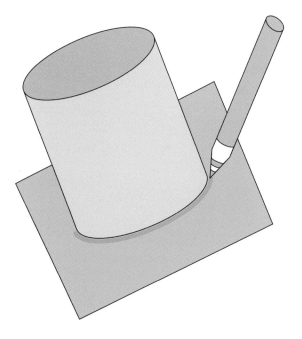

# Finish It

**1** Follow the manufacturer's directions to remove all traces of the erasable marker, or brush away any remaining dressmaker's tracing paper lines.

**2** To even out your stitches and make your patches look nice and neat, you can block them (page 59).

**3** If you have enough open space around your embroidered motif, you can frame it by sewing other stitches along the edge.

# Use It

## Attach the Patch

**1** To attach the patch to an object, such as a barrette, baseball cap, or backpack, squeeze a small amount of fabric glue onto the back of the patch, and spread it carefully to the edges. Try not to use too much glue, or it will be messy and come through to the front side of the embroidery.

**2** Use your fingers to press the patch onto the object, and lay it flat to dry. If you're attaching it to a rounded object, like a barrette, hold the patch in place for a few minutes so that the glue will attach securely at all points.

## Make a Hanging Ornament

Cut a piece of ribbon, rickrack, or seam binding about 6˝–8˝. Fold it in half and use fabric glue to attach it to the back of the patch.

**Note:** *Make sure you glue the ribbon to the top point of the design so that it will hang with the top side up.*

> **TIP**
>
> *If you don't want to make a felt patch, you can embroider any of these designs directly on other surfaces, such as your blue jeans, pillowcases, jackets, or T-shirts.*

# How to Make It Yours

Stitch Guide

| THE LOOK | THE STITCH |
|---|---|
| Thin lines (straight or curved) | Stem stitch, backstitch, chain stitch |
| Short lines | Single straight stitches |
| Zigzag lines | Featherstitch, backstitch, running stitch |
| Solid shapes with one color | Satin stitch (or sew stem or chain stitches very closely together to make a solid area of color) |
| Small dots and circles | French knots, satin stitch, spider web stitch |
| Small ovals | Bullion knots, satin stitch, woven bar stitch |
| Rectangles | Woven bar stitch, satin stitch |
| Flowers | Straight stitch, spider web stitch, lazy daisy stitch |
| Leaves | Satin stitch, single chain stitches, woven bar stitch |

# Motifs

A motif is a single small drawing or image that can be a design all by itself or can make up part of a larger design. **GEOMETRIC SHAPES LIKE CIRCLES, SQUARES, AND TRIANGLES ARE VERY SIMPLE MOTIFS.**

A flower composed of center, petals, and stem is a more complicated motif. In embroidery, you can make up your own motifs or copy ones that you see in other places, such as on books, wallpaper, rugs, or fabric. Several motifs are provided in Templates and Motifs (pages 122–126).

Some motifs are used by many different cultures throughout the world, and some are unique to a specific culture. Here is a list of some traditional motifs, with explanations of what they have come to symbolize.

## Circles

A symbol for the sun, which represents life, warmth, and the never-ending cycle of life because the sun rises and sets every day.

## Trees

A symbol for birth, life, and death. A common motif called the Tree of Life features birds, animals, fruits, and flowers.

## Flowers and Fruit

A symbol of the bounty of the harvest and the importance of the earth as a source of growing things.

## Curves or Crescent Shapes

A curved symbol can stand for animals with horns, like deer and cows. A crescent can also represent the moon. Two curves turned inward to face each other become a heart, the symbol of love.

## Crosses

A cross made with both lines the same length, like a plus sign, can symbolize stars and the heavens.

# Finding Embroidery Ideas

One of the coolest things about embroidery is that you can make almost any design with it—from a simple shape to a fancy picture—but sometimes it's hard to decide where to start. Ideas are all around, if you know where to look.

## Ideas from Nature

Take a walk with a notebook for jotting down ideas. Pay attention to birds and other animals, the shapes of leaves and flowers, the textures of plants and rocks, the colors in the sky and water, everything around you.

## Ideas from Books and Magazines

Look in books and magazines for decorative borders or fancy type (called fonts) you can trace, or things you might not see on your nature walk—like a lion or an alien. There are books and websites with small designs called clip art. Often these simple drawings are free for anyone to use. Search by theme, like holidays or sports, and you can transfer the designs to fabric for stitching.

## Ideas from Family Life

Think about your family's interests. If you are wild about soccer, embroider a soccer ball on your gym bag. If your mom and dad love ballet, embroider a ballerina on a patch for them. Alternatively, embroider a picture of your pet on a pillow for a couch.

## Ideas from Doodling

Turn your doodles into artwork. Take a simple shape like a circle or diamond and repeat it over and over to build your own pattern. If you overlap geometric shapes or place small ones inside larger ones, your pattern will become more complex.

# Embroidery Explorations

Embroidery has been practiced for thousands of years. To see samples made long ago and far away, visit history, art, textile, and folk museums. YOUR LOCAL HISTORICAL SOCIETY MAY EVEN HAVE SAMPLES OF EMBROIDERY that were made in your town. If no one in your family knows how to embroider and you need help, ask a teacher or librarian if they know someone who can assist you. Also, try your local needlework, craft, or fabric stores for classes.

START YOUR OWN EMBROIDERY CLUB SO YOU AND YOUR FRIENDS CAN SHARE YOUR SKILLS AND IDEAS. Long ago, these kinds of clubs were called sewing circles or quilting bees and were very popular; each neighborhood had one or more groups.

Visit some of the fun sites on the Internet that feature information about embroidery and embroidery techniques, such as:

needlenthread.com  

cross-stitching.com  

doverpublications.com  

freeembroiderystuff.com  

historic-deerfield.org  

needleworksamplers.com  

needlecrafter.com  

feelingstitchy.com

Check your local library or bookstore for more information too. There are thousands of stitches you can learn, after you master the basics.

REMEMBER, YOU ARE THE BOSS WHEN IT COMES TO YOUR EMBROIDERY. If you like the way your embroidery looks with your stitch and design choices, then you are doing it right.

# Glossary

**Erasable fabric marker:** marker specially designed so the marks are removable. Several types of markers are available. Each works a little differently, so be sure to follow the instructions.

**Card stock:** heavyweight paper

**Dressmaker's transfer paper:** graphite and wax-free transfer paper used for transferring line drawings to fabric for embroidering over. It comes in many colors. Choose a color that will show up on your fabric.

**Embroidery floss:** mercerized cotton thread composed of 6 strands. It comes in hundreds of colors.

**Felt:** nonwoven fabric made of wool or acrylic fibers that are pressed together. It does not fray when cut and is perfect for beginning stitchers.

**Perle cotton:** a mercerized thread with a nice sheen frequently used for embroidery.

**Persian wool:** wool thread commonly used for needlepoint and embroidery. It has 3 strands.

**Plastic canvas:** lightweight plastic with regularly spaced holes resembling an even weave mesh. It is used as a foundation for needlepoint. It is rigid and a great surface for beginning stitchers.

**Remnant:** a leftover piece of fabric that can be used for other projects.

**Skein:** a length of yarn or thread that is wound in an orderly fashion. Skeins are usually held together with paper labels.

# Patterns and Motifs

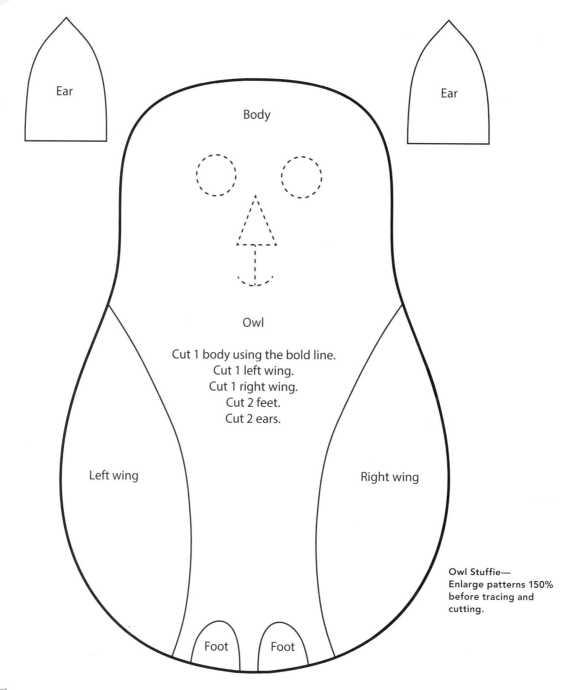

Ear

Ear

Body

Owl

Cut 1 body using the bold line.
Cut 1 left wing.
Cut 1 right wing.
Cut 2 feet.
Cut 2 ears.

Left wing

Right wing

Owl Stuffie—
Enlarge patterns 150%
before tracing and
cutting.

Foot    Foot

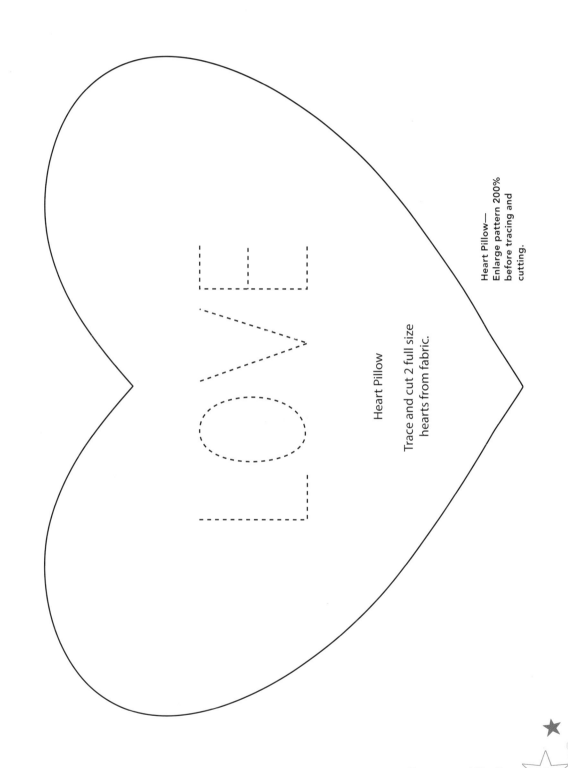

Heart Pillow

Trace and cut 2 full size hearts from fabric.

Heart Pillow—
Enlarge pattern 200%
before tracing and
cutting.

The Amazing Stitching Handbook for Kids

The Amazing Stitching Handbook for Kids

You Rock!

PEACE

LOVE

The Amazing Stitching Handbook for Kids

# About the Author

Photo by Sarah Zimmerman

*Kristin Nicholas* grew up in northern New Jersey in a creative family of five girls. Throughout her childhood, she sewed, quilted, crocheted, and embroidered. She studied textiles and clothing design at the University of Delaware, Oregon State University, and Colorado State University, where she taught herself to knit by hand. For 16 years, she was creative director at Classic Elite Yarns. She has been designing for the knitting and needlework industry for over 30 years. Kristin is a knitting expert on PBS's *Knit and Crochet Now* and has appeared on *Martha Stewart TV* and many DIY television shows. She teaches online stitching classes on Creativebug and Craftsy. She is the author of numerous books, including *Colorful Stitchery* (Roost Books, 2014) and *Crafting a Colorful Home* (Roost Books, 2015). Kristin lives with her husband, Mark, and daughter, Julia, at Leyden Glen Farm, a working sheep farm in western Massachusetts. She writes the popular blog *Getting Stitched on the Farm*. You can see more of her work on her website, kristinnicholas.com.

## Sources for Supplies

**COTTON EMBROIDERY FLOSS AND PERLE COTTON**
Available at craft, sewing, and quilting stores. Major brands include DMC and Anchor.

**WOOL FOR STITCHING**
Paternayan Persian wool (sacoriverdyehouse.com/site)

Appleton Crewel Wool (kristinnicholas.com)

**WOOL FELT**
A Child's Dream (achildsdream.com)

**WOOL AND COTTON DYES**
Dharma Trading Company (dharmatrading.com).

**FABRIC PAINT**
Available at craft stores. Popular brands include Plaid and Duncan.

**LESLEY RILEY'S TAP TRANSFER ARTIST PAPER**
C&T Publishing (ctpub.com)

# FunStitch
## STUDIO

**FunStitch Studio** books are written and designed specifically with kids, tweens, and teens in mind!

"Every time I finish a project, **I get so excited**, because I feel like I can do **anything!**"
—— *Annalise, age 12* ——

The text and projects are age appropriate and *nurture the love of handmade* in budding sewists, quilters, embroiderers, and fashion designers.

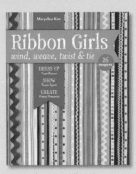

by Maryellen Kim

by Ali Benyon

by Judith Cressy

by Allison Nicoll

See the complete list of FunStitch Studio titles at ctpub.com/ funstitch-studio

an imprint of C&T Publishing